OUT OF NOWHERE

MICHAEL M. GUNTER

Out of Nowhere

The Kurds of Syria in Peace and War

HURST & COMPANY, LONDON

First published in the United Kingdom in 2014 by
C. Hurst & Co. (Publishers) Ltd.,
41 Great Russell Street, London, WC1B 3PL
© Michael M. Gunter, 2014
All rights reserved.
Printed in India

Distributed in the United States, Canada and Latin America by
Oxford University Press, 198 Madison Avenue, New York, NY 10016,
United States of America

A Cataloguing-in-Publication data record for this book
is available from the British Library.

ISBN: 978-1-84904-435-6

www.hurstpublishers.com

This book is printed using paper from registered sustainable
and managed sources.

Credit for the map: Syrian Kurds (Harriet Montgomery [Allsopp], *The Kurds of
Syria: An Existence Denied*, Berlin: European Center for Kurdish Studies)

Dedicated to my dear wife Judy, my love and support

CONTENTS

ACRONYMS AND ABBREVIATIONS

AKP	*Adalet ve Kalkinma Partisi* or AK Partisi (Justice and Development Party) [Turkey]
AQI	Al-Qaeda in Iraq
BDP	*Baris ve Demokrasi Partisi* (Peace and Democracy Party) [Turkey]
CCC	Central Coordinating Committee (PYD)
CHP	*Cumhuriyet Halk Partisi* (Republican Peoples Party) [Turkey]
CIA	Central Intelligence Agency [USA]
DTK	*Demokratik Toplum Kongresi* (Democratic Society Congress) [Turkey]
DTP	*Demokratik Toplum Partisi* (Democratic Society Party) [Turkey]
EU	European Union
EUTCC	EU Turkey Civic Commission
FDI	Foreign direct investment
FGM	Female genital mutilation
FSA	Free Syrian Army
GAP	*Guneydogu Anadolu Projesi* (Southeast Anatolia Project) [Turkey]
HPG	*Hezen Parastina Gel* (Peoples Defence Force) [PKK]
ICG	International Crisis Group
IDP	Internally Displaced Person
ISIS	Islamic State of Iraq and Syria [al-Sham/Levant]
KCK	*Koma Civaken Kurdistan* (Kurdistan Communities Union) [PKK]
KDP	Kurdistan Democratic Party [Iraq]

KDPS	Kurdish Democratic Party [Syria]
KGK	Kongra Gel (Kurdistan Peoples Congress) [PKK]
KNAS	Kurdistan National Assembly of Syria
KNC	Kurdish National Council/Coalition [Syria]
KNK	*Kongra Netewiya Kurdistan* (Kurdistan National Congress) [PKK]
KRG	Kurdistan Regional Government [Iraq]
MHP	*Milliyetci Haraket Partisi* (Nationalist Action Party) [Turkey]
MIT	*Milli Istihbarat Teshilati* (National Intelligence Organization) [Turkey]
MP	Member of Parliament
NATO	North Atlantic Treaty Organization
NRT	Naliya Radio and Television (KRG)
OPC	Operation Provide Comfort
PCWK	Peoples Council of Western Kurdistan (PYD)
PKK	*Partiya Karkaren Kurdistan* (Kurdistan Workers Party) [Turkey]
PUK	*Patriotic Union of Kurdistan* [Iraq]
PYD	*Partiya Yekita ya Demokratik* (Democratic Union Party) [Syria] [PKK]
SALSRA	Syria Accountability and Lebanese Sovereignty Restoration Act [USA]
SCP	Syrian Communist Party
SKDCP	Syrian Kurdish Democratic Concord Party/*Wifaq*
SNC	Syrian National Coalition (November 2012–)
SNC	Syrian National Council (August 2011–November 2012)
TAL	Transitional Administrative Law [Iraq]
TEV-DEM	*Tevgera Civaka Demokratik* (Movement for a Democratic Society/Democratic Popular Movement) (PYD)
UAR	United Arab Republic (Egypt & Syria: 1958–1961)
UN	United Nations
YPG	*Yekineyen Parastina Gel* (Peoples Defence Units) (PYD)

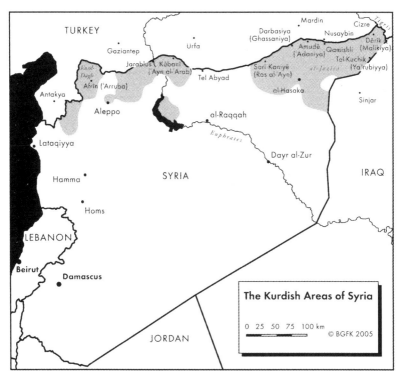

Map of the Kurdish areas of Syria

INTRODUCTION

On 19 July 2012 the previously almost unheard of Syrian Kurds suddenly emerged as a potential game changer in the Syrian civil war and what its aftermath might hold for the future in the Middle East when in an attempt to consolidate their increasingly desperate position, government troops were abruptly pulled out of the major Kurdish areas. The Kurds in Syria had suddenly become autonomous, a situation that also gravely affected neighbouring Turkey and the virtually independent Kurdistan Regional Government (KRG) in Iraq. Indeed, the precipitous rise of the Kurds in Syria bid to become a tipping point that might help change the artificial borders of the Middle East established after the First World War following the notorious Sykes-Picot Agreement.

Although there are a few earlier studies of the Syrian Kurds,[1] no other book has tackled these important recent events. Thus, after several brief chapters to set the stage, the main purpose of this book will be to interpret these potentially momentous events. In so doing, this book will also visit the Sunni-Shiite sectarian fault-line and the future of such regional states involved in the Syrian cataclysm as Turkey and Iraq, as well as the role of the United States, among others.

Kurdistan, or the Land of the Kurds, straddles the mountainous borders in the Middle East where Turkey, Iran, Iraq and Syria converge, while the Kurds famously constitute the largest nation in the world without their own independent state. Nevertheless, in recent years the Kurds living in Iraq, Turkey and Iran have frequently been heard from, but until 19 July 2012, when the Syrian civil war suddenly resulted in their autonomy and even possible independence, those living in Syria had been virtually invisible. The purpose of this book is also to help explain this near vacuum of information and rectify it. Such an endeavour is all the more important given the crucial middle role the Kurds are playing in the Syrian civil war, a struggle with deep implications for the future of the Middle East.

Nobody really knows how many Kurds live in Syria because the Kurds exaggerate their numbers, while the government undercounts them to de-emphasise the size of the problem. In addition, a significant number of Kurds have assimilated or chosen to identify themselves in other ways. Nevertheless, a reasonable estimate might be that approximately 10 per cent or slightly more than 2.2 million Kurds may live in Syria, a much smaller number than in Turkey, Iraq and Iran.[2] Although the largest ethnic minority in Syria, the Kurds live in three non-contiguous areas and have been much less successfully organised and developed than in the other three states. For many years the repressive Syrian government of Hafez Assad also sought to maintain an Arab belt between its Kurds and those in Turkey and Iraq. This Arab belt artificially separated the Kurds in Syria from their ethnic kin and in many cases from actual blood relatives across the border in Turkey and Iraq, uprooted many Syrian Kurds and deprived them of their livelihoods.

Many Kurds in Syria have even been denied Syrian citizenship. In 1962, Decree 93 classified some 120,000 Kurds as *ajanib* (foreigners) who could not vote, own property or work in government jobs. This status has been inherited and thus the number of *ajanib* may now be as high as 300,000 or more. In addition, some 75,000 other Syrian Kurds became known as *maktoumeen* (concealed). As such, they had virtually no civil rights and were even worse off than the *ajanib*. Furthermore, a government decree in September 1992 prohibited the registration of children with Kurdish first names. Kurdish cultural centres, bookshops and similar activities have also been banned. Indeed, some have suspected that in return for the sanctuary given to the Kurdistan Workers Party (PKK) in Syria for many years, the PKK—a Kurdish insurgent group fighting against Turkey since 1984—kept the lid on Syrian Kurdish unrest. For all these reasons, therefore, little was heard about the Kurds in Syria.

The fall of Saddam Hussein in March 2003 and the eventual recognition by the new Iraqi state of the KRG as a virtually independent Kurdish state in northern Iraq helped begin to change this situation. The very existence of the newly empowered Kurds in Iraq began to encourage the Kurds living in other states such as Syria and even challenged the artificial borders created by the Sykes-Picot Agreement in 1916. In March

2004, Kurdish rioting broke out at a football match in Qamishli, Syria— a city considered by many to be the notional capital of Syrian (Western) Kurdistan, also known by the Kurds as Rojava or 'direction from where the sun sets'. Since then, the atmosphere has remained tense. Renewed rioting occurred a year later in Aleppo following the killing of Maashouq al-Khaznawi, an outspoken Kurdish cleric critical of the regime. Many Kurds blamed Haznawi's murder on the Syrian government.

Within days of becoming president of the KRG in June 2005, Massoud Barzani demanded that the Syrian Kurds be granted their rights peacefully. Seldom in the past had Kurdish groups outside Syria thus spoken. This was because previously the Syrian government had allowed these other or foreign Kurds sanctuary in Syria as a tool against such regional enemies as Turkey and Iraq, as well as a way of keeping the lid on Syria's own potential Kurdish problem by having these foreign Kurds ignore the Syrian Kurds in return for the sanctuary Syria was giving them. Indeed, Jalal Talabani's Patriotic Union of Kurdistan (PUK)—one of the two main Kurdish parties in Iraq—was established in Damascus on 1 June 1975, while Massoud Barzani's Kurdistan Democratic Party (KDP), the other main Iraqi Kurdish party, enjoyed sanctuary there from Saddam Hussein for many years. Given the new situation of a virtually independent KRG after the fall of Saddam Hussein in March 2003, the situation changed and foreign Kurds began to speak up for their long forgotten ethnic kin in Syria.

In addition, on 16 October 2005, an emboldened domestic Syrian opposition consisting of such disparate groups as the Muslim Brotherhood and the Communists issued a 'Damascus Declaration for Democratic National Change'. Among many other points, the declaration called for 'A just democratic solution to the Kurdish issue in Syria, in a manner that guarantees the complete equality of Syrian Kurdish citizens, with regard to nationality rights, culture, learning the national language, and other constitutional […] rights.'[3]

The forced Syrian troop withdrawal from Lebanon following the assassination of the former Lebanese Prime Minister Rafiq Hariri in February 2005, the strong UN Security Council response leading to the Mehlis Report on apparent Syrian involvement in the affair and the US occupation of neighbouring Iraq also presented grave international challenges to the Syrian regime. Although Bashar Assad—who had succeeded his father when he died in 2000—originally indicated that he was willing to entertain reforms, he soon reneged on this implicit promise, probably because he feared that it would open the floodgates of demands leading to his ousting. The Syrian civil war that began in March 2011, however, perhaps indicated that Assad was doomed whether he entertained reform or opted for further crackdowns.

The first chapter of this book will deal with the background by examining the Syrian colonial legacy as a French mandate of the League of Nations, followed by Syrian independence in 1946. Here we will touch on the roles of the famous Bedir Khan brothers who practically invented Kurdish nationalism in the 1920s; Osman Sabri, one of the first modern Kurdish leaders in Syria; Hajo Agha, the most influential tribal leader of his generation, but nevertheless a harbinger of Kurdish nationalism in Syria; Khoybun, the first transnational Kurdish political party; and the first leaders of independent Syria, some of whom were actually Kurds, among other events.

The second chapter, entitled simply 'The Forgotten', will analyse how the Syrian Arab government tried to reduce the status of the Kurds in Syria to that of the invisible. Specifically, the notorious report published in 1963 by the Syrian Arab official Muhammad Talab Hilal on how to excise 'the cancerous Kurdish tumour' from the Syrian body politic, along with such other initiatives as Decree 93 concerning the *ajanib* and *maktoumeen* as well as the Arab Belt (*al-Hizam al-Arabi*) to create an artificial cordon sanitaire of Syrian Arabs between foreign Kurds living in Turkey and Iraq on the one hand and those living in Syria on the other, among other measures, will be analysed. This chapter will also discuss how the proliferation of small Kurdish political parties beginning in the 1960s also played a significant role in the Kurds becoming virtually forgotten. Chapter 3 on 'Women' will further examine why the Kurds in Syria became the forgotten.

'Transnational Actors', the following chapter, will analyse state and non-state actors such as Turkey, Iraq, the United States and others, on the one hand, and the PKK, KRG and its leading political parties, the KDP and PUK, among others, on the other. The ensuing two chapters will then go into further detail on 'The KRG Model', which is one that is more moderate, and 'The PKK Model', which presents a more radical ideal to emulate for the emerging Syrian Kurds. Next will come a chapter on what might be called the six stages of US foreign policy towards the Kurds overall, with the final stage devoted to those in Syria in particular.

The next chapter, 'Prelude', will examine which events led to the sudden autonomy thrust upon the Kurds in July 2012 when the beleaguered Syrian government suddenly pulled most of its troops and infrastructure out of the Kurdish areas in north-eastern Syria. First we will analyse the *Serhildan* (Uprising) of March 2004 that was ignited by a football match in Qamishli, and how it presented the Kurds in Syria with their own national narrative for the first time. The assassination of Mishaal Tammo, the much-admired leader of the Kurdish Future Movement in October 2011, proved to be another prelude to the sudden autonomy thrust upon the Kurds. Finally, of course, the Syrian civil war constitutes the most essential prelude that will be considered. How has this incredibly complicated and continuing struggle to the death played out regarding the Kurds and how is it most likely to affect their future?

Thus, in the following chapter on 'Autonomy' we will analyse the sudden rise of Salih Muslim (Muhammed) and his Democratic Union Party (PYD)—which was created by the PKK and remains affiliated to it—the extremely complicated and deadly fighting and attempts at negotiating between factions of the Free Syrian Army (FSA) or Syrian opposition like the Jabhat al-Nusra jihadists/Salafists on the one hand and the PYD and numerous other Kurdish groups loosely organised as the Kurdish National Council on the other, as well as murderous Kurdish infighting.

Finally, the last chapter will examine 'The Future' which might have many possibilities depending on the outcome of the civil war in Syria. The Kurds in Syria after all remain relatively weak despite their recent gains both domestically and regionally. Thus, if the Assad regime or its opposition wins a complete victory, either can be expected to seek to reduce the rights of Syria's Kurds once again. On the other hand, if neither side wins a total victory and Syria descends into a collection of *de facto* statelets, the Kurds in Syria might become one of them or seek to be annexed by Turkey or the KRG. However, the PYD, by far the most powerful Kurdish political party in Syria, claims that it will institute 'democratic autonomy', a new type of bottom-up civil society organisation that has been adumbrated by Abdullah Ocalan, the leader of the PKK, and would also include non-Kurds. How realistic would this be?

1

BACKGROUND

Although Syria is an ancient land, the modern state only dates from the French mandate established in 1920. The earlier concept of Greater Syria (*Bilad al-Sham*) had been a much larger one that also included today's Lebanon, Jordan and what was then known as Palestine, which is today's Israel, the West Bank and the Gaza Strip. Indeed some Arab nationalists would even include modern Iraq so that Greater Syria would denote the united Fertile Crescent. Thus, this study of the Kurds in Syria largely begins with the French mandate as any earlier mention of Syria could easily be misleading. In addition, since there were no separate states of Turkey, Iraq and Syria until the collapse of the Ottoman Empire after the First World War, the Kurds of those future states simply lived in the Ottoman Empire. The concept of the Kurds in Syria could not be meaningful until the French mandate was created and even later, after failed Kurdish uprisings during the 1920s in Turkey forced many Kurds to leave that country for Syria.

Among pan-Kurdish nationalists, Syrian Kurdistan is often referred to as Western Kurdistan or Rojava (the direction of the setting sun). Since this region contains the country's most fertile areas and is also home to most of its oil reserves, the Kurdish-populated areas of Syria are a prize well worth struggling over.[1]

During the past century it might be said that the Kurds in Syria have suffered under a form of sequential triple colonialism: first, the Ottoman Empire until 1918; then the French until 1946;[2] and subsequently the Arabs once Syria gained its independence. Furthermore, after it came to power in 1963, the now moribund Baathist party proved even more hostile toward the Kurds. However, this heritage has not been completely negative as the Ottomans in many ways reserved priority for their Muslim subjects of which the Kurds constituted a part, and on occasion the French actually showed favouritism towards such minorities as the Kurds in order to rule the Sunni Arab majority. Thus, it might be argued that assimilationist and denialist Arab colonialism has most exploited the Kurds in Syria.

Kurdish roots in Syria

As testimony to Kurdish roots in Syria, the huge Crusader castle Krak des Chevaliers in the Alawite mountains between Homs and Tartus is called in Arabic Hisn al-Akrad or Castle of the Kurds. Salah al-Din (Saladin), the most famous Kurd of all, is buried in the great mosque in Damascus. Kurd Dagh or Kurd Mountain north-west of Aleppo (also referred to as Afrin after its main city) remains one of the three distinct and separate Kurdish areas in Syria, while Kobani (Ain al-Arab) in the north central area of Syria and Hasaka (Hesice) or Jazira (Island, in reference to its lying between the Euphrates and Tigris Rivers) in the northeastern part of Syria constitute the other two separate and distinct Kurdish areas in Syria. Kurd Dagh and Kobani are contiguous to Kurdish-populated areas in Turkey, while part of Hasaka (Jazira) borders Kurdish areas in both Turkey and Iraq in the area the French called le Bec de Canard, or the 'Duck's Beak' in reference to its relatively long, narrow shape that juts between Turkey and Iraq. Indeed Cizre, once the capital of the Kurdish emirate of Botan and now situated in Turkey, lies only some twenty miles from the Syrian border. Qamishli—with a population of 184,231 according to the 2004 census, but now much larger—is the largest Kurdish city in Syria and, as noted in the Introduction, is often considered the *de facto* capital of Western (Syrian) Kurdistan. It borders on the Turkish city of Nusaybin in the province of Hasaka (Jazira). In addition, maybe 20 per cent of the Kurds in Syria also live in the predominantly Kurdish quarters of Aleppo (Sheikh Maqsood, Ashrafiyya and Shar) and Damascus (Zorava [aka Wadi al-Mashari], Jabal al-Rizz and Rukn al-Din).

Almost all of the Syrian Kurds speak the Kurdish language/dialect of Kurmanji. Many have relatives in Turkey as the present international border was only drawn following the First World War, largely along the lines fashioned by the secretive British-French Sykes-Picot Agreement of 1916, which became a byword for British-French imperialist control of the Middle East and manipulation of the Kurds.

Kurdish situation before the current civil war

Many Kurds living in the Syrian province of Hasaka (Jazira) originally fled to the region from Turkey following the failure of the Sheikh Said Rebellion in 1925 and subsequent Kurdish uprisings in Turkey.[3] As Wadie Jwaideh has pointed out, developments in Turkey had a profound influence on the Kurdish situation in Syria. This was true for both the urban Kurdish population and the rural tribes. 'The newly drawn frontier line did not mean much at the time to the Kurdish tribesmen in the northern frontier regions of the country, for although the new frontier in many cases placed members of the same tribe under two different administrations, French and Turkish, it separated but did not actually sever the two segments.'[4] However, this situation regarding the Turkish origin of some Syrian Kurds provided the Syrian rationale for the disenfranchisement of many of these Kurds in modern Syria, which began with the French mandate under the League of Nations following the First World War and the removal of the short-lived rule of Faisal as king. After much acrimony, a French-Turkish agreement arbitrarily made the Baghdad railway line that ran between Mosul in Iraq and Aleppo in Syria the present border between most of Turkey and Syria after it crossed the Iraqi-Syrian boundary. Indeed even today many Kurds in Turkey and Syria who live on either side of the border do not refer to themselves as coming from those states. Rather, for the Kurds of Turkey, Syria is *Bin Xhet* (below the line), and for the Kurds of Syria, Turkey is *Ser Xhet* (above the line).

Although the League of Nations' concept of mandates began as simply the old hag of colonialism putting on a fig leaf and calling itself mandate, in time it began to develop as a genuine pathway to independence. Thus, the British mandate of Iraq technically won its freedom as early as 1932, while Syria achieved it in 1946. Under the French mandate, underdeveloped and nascent Kurdish national identity was not deemed a threat such as the more mature Arab identity held. Thus, the Kurds in Syria enjoyed many political and cultural rights as illustrated by the rise of a modest civil society consisting of political and social organisations, the legal authorisation of Kurdish language use and publications, and Kurdish recruitment

9

into both the governmental administration and the military. A number of Kurdish tribes and *aghas* (landlords) also supported French rule because decentralisation did not seem to challenge their traditional authority. On the other hand, it is also true that some Kurds joined uprisings or rebellions against the French mandate. During the 1930s these Kurds lobbied for an autonomous government in part as a reaction to the French attempt to settle Sunni Arabs in the area and as a result of the traditional Kurdish disdain for centralised government.

By comparison with Iraq and Turkey, however, a sense of Kurdish national identity developed more slowly in Syria in part because of the divisions between tribes and *aghas* who were usually not motivated by nationalist concerns. Urban and rural Kurdish divisions also inhibited Kurdish national awareness; domestic leaders continued to arise from urban and merchant families whose origin stemmed from the Ottoman period and who thus possessed minimal Kurdish identity. Indeed many urban Kurds were almost entirely Arabicised, Muhammad Kurd Ali (1876–1953), a noted intellectual, and Khalid Bakdash (1912–95), who became the leader of the Syrian Communist Party during the 1930s, being primary examples. Rural Kurds living in the Jazira and Kurd Dagh had little in common with such urbanites, especially given their strong socio-economic differences. Furthermore, given how new the ideas of Syrian nationalism and statehood were, most Kurds who were motivated by their Kurdish identity at first thought of themselves less as Syrian Kurds and more as members of the wider pan-Kurdish nation. On the other hand, Sheikh Ahmad Kuftaru (1921–2004) made no attempt to hide his Kurdish origins, serving in Damascus as the Grand Mufti of Syria for forty years until his death, by 'being a very popular spiritual leader among the Kurds and Sunni Arabs at the same time, […] rejecting the idea of political Islam', and acting as 'an intermediary between the state and the Syrian Kurds'.[5]

Among the most prominent leaders of the Syrian Kurds during the French mandate era were the Bedir Khan brothers (Thurayya, Jaladet and Kamuran) who originally came from Cizre in Turkey. The brothers were grandsons of the famous Bedir Khan Beg (c.1800–1868), the last emir of the Kurdish emirate of Botan in what is today south-eastern Turkey. Thus, his grandsons were of princely descent. Each grandson became a famous Kurdish intellectual in the cause of Kurdish nationalism and was also a noted figure in Kurdish literature.

Jaladet Bedir Khan (1893–1951), for example, helped to develop a Kurdish alphabet with Latin letters, while Kamuran Bedir Khan (1895–1978) became an author, editor and professor teaching Kurdish at the Ecole des Langues Orientales in Paris, where today's prominent scholar of Kurdish literature Joyce Blau was one of his students. During the 1960s Kamuran also served as a spokesman for Mulla Mustafa Barzani, the famous Iraqi Kurdish nationalist/tribal leader, at the United Nations. Thurayya Bedir Khan (1883–1938) published a bilingual Kurdish-Turkish journal in Istanbul called *Kurdistan* after the Young Turk coup in 1908 and was one of the original members of the transnational Kurdish political party Khoybun (literally, Be Yourself, or Independence) that was formed in Bhamdoun in Lebanon in October 1927 by Kurdish intellectuals of aristocratic background living in exile.

Khoybun had the close co-operation of the Armenian nationalist Dashnak party and also enjoyed some initial support from France, particularly in the Jazira area where the French needed strong local backing to implement their own rule. Jaladet Bedir Khan served as Khoybun's first president, along with several other prominent figures. Khoybun's permanent headquarters were established in Aleppo with French acquiescence.

Khoybun sought to establish a strong Kurdish national liberation movement with a trained fighting force that would not depend on the traditional tribal leaders, although Hajo Agha, who originally had been expelled from Turkey in 1926 and was the leader of the powerful Heverkan tribal confederation of some twenty separate tribes, was also an important leader. Osman Sabri (1905–93), who later created the first Kurdish party in Syria, the Kurdish Democratic Party, in 1957, also hailed from tribal origins, and had fled from Turkey. He too played an important role in Khoybun.

Most famously perhaps, Khoybun instigated the unsuccessful Ararat uprising of the Kurds in Turkey from 1927 to 1930 under the military leadership of General Ihsan Nuri Pasha, a former commander in the Ottoman army and Kurdish negotiator during the peace conferences after the First World War. Eventually, however, Iran helped Turkey crush the rebellion, while France tightened its restrictions on the party in response to Turkish pressure.

Although Khoybun failed to achieve its immediate goals in Syria or Turkey, its nationalist ideology had a permanent effect on many Kurds in Syria by bringing them into belated contact with nationalist concepts already widespread among the Arabs and Turks. Thus, the Kurdish nation was cast in a primordial light as dating back to some distant point in history and merely in need of having its ancient national identity revived. Although such an essentialist view was largely a myth, Khoybun did play a constructive role by helping to begin the process of creating or inventing Kurdish nationalism.[6] However, the failure of Khoybun's armed struggle led most Kurds in Syria to abandon it at the time in favour of political and cultural activity.

Indeed, such activities had already begun before the defeat of Khoybun. In 1928, for example, five Kurds were elected to the Syrian parliament where they lobbied for Kurdish being made the official language of the Kurdish areas in Syria and for the creation of a Kurdish educational system. This proposal failed to be implemented owing to the lack of qualified instructors and adequate pedagogical materials. The French also turned down a demand by these same Kurdish parliamentarians for Kurdish administrative autonomy, with the argument that the Kurds did not constitute a religious minority like the Alawites and the Druzes and that the Kurdish areas were not contiguous. A proposal to create a Kurdish humanitarian and charitable organisation in Jazira also failed.

However, Sexmus Hesen Cegerxwin (1903–84) proved a vibrant and popular patriotic poet and Jaladet Bedir Khan established *Hawar* (The Calling), a monthly journal to promote a popular literature and teaching materials in Kurdish. Hajo Agha of the Heverkan tribal confederation also played a significant role in *Hawar*, publishing an article in it that was important in promoting Kurdish education among tribal leaders. He also distributed books in Kurdish to visitors at his home in Jazira, strongly encouraged the teaching of the language and, despite his continuing tribal ties, displayed a Kurdish flag in front of his home.

In addition, to treating social and cultural issues, *Hawar* also dealt with Kurdish linguistics, grammar and dialects as well as introducing a Latin script for the Kurdish language. Although *Hawar* only ran from 1932 to 1937 when the French authorities banned it, the journal played an important role in the unification of Kurdish dialects and the creation of a standardised Kurdish language. By opening up a serious dialogue among the different elements in Syrian Kurdish society, *Hawar* contributed importantly to a sense of Kurdish identity. Nevertheless, widespread Kurdish identity among Kurds in Syria remained barely nascent.

Therefore, at this point it would be useful to turn to an analysis of the failed antecedents (approximately up to 1938) of contemporary Kurdish nationalism by Martin Strohmeier.[7] Although *Failed Antecedents of Contemporary Kurdish Nationalism* might have been a better title for the book, Strohmeier is concerned with the attempts to create Kurdish nationalism in this earlier period up through the 1930s, as well as analysing why these efforts at the time seemingly failed. Thus, his treatise offers to English-only readers a wealth of material previously available only in pieces discussed by such scholars as Robert Olson[8] and Martin van Bruinessen,[9] among others.

Using short, pithy chapters, Strohmeier divides his work into three sections.[10] Part One analyses the attempts before the First World War by aspiring Kurdish nationalists to awaken their would-be compatriots to their cause through newspapers. Tellingly, however, General Ihsan Nuri Pasha, the Kurdish leader of the Khoybun-led Ararat revolt in the late 1920s referred to above, related in his memoirs that 'a newspaper written in Kurdish called *Agri* was distributed at Ararat but, due to the lack of paper, there were few copies' (p. 191). Part Two deals with the Bedir Khan brothers' (Thurayya, Kamuran and Jaladet) development in the 1920s of a Kurdish movement in exile (mainly in Syria), the failure of their transnational Kurdish party Khoybun and the negation of Kurdish nationalism by Shukru Mehmed Sekban. The third and final part analyses a little known novel (*Der Adler von Kurdistan*) co-authored in the 1930s by Kamuran Bedir Khan, which failed to become a Kurdish national epic but does give valuable insights into what he saw as the characteristics of the imagined Kurdish nation.

These early would-be Kurdish nationalists grappled with many problems including the nature of the Kurdish relationship with the Ottomans, Arabs and Europeans, and the primitive state of affairs in Kurdistan. 'All Kurds were deeply if variously enmeshed in social, ideological, economic and personal relations with the Turks. [...] These bonds hampered the development of a self-assertive, robust and distinct Kurdish identity' (p. 54). In addition, the Kurdish 'language was a shambles, not fit for education or literature; their culture was backward, and their history was a mystery' (p. 45). Furthermore, 'a language-factor potentially more divisive than dialects was the problem presented by Turkish speakers among the Kurds' (p. 61).[11]

Then, following the First World War and the subsequent rush to create nation-states in the Middle East, the Kurds had no one to counter the appeal to Muslim loyalty of Mustafa Kemal (Ataturk). 'Kurdish leaders such as Serif Pasha appeared to be traitors willing to sign away the fatherland to the Armenian enemies' (p. 70). 'The making of their (Turkish) nation was to depend on the unmaking of any plans the Kurds had had for their own nation' (p. 84). In addition, by helping the Turks rid 'the area of Armenians, the Kurds had unwittingly forfeited their historical status and value to the Turks as counterweights to the Armenians' (p. 87).

On the other hand, *Mem u Zin*—the Kurdish national epic dating from the seventeenth century—'constitutes the backbone of the argument that Kurds are a nation capable of attaining a high level of civilization, and possessing a language which can yield great literature [...] The epic lends itself astonishingly well to the exigencies of national identity building because of its many-faceted appeal to diverse groups in Kurdish society [...] and has become almost a "Declaration of Independence" in Kurdish history' (p. 27). Addressing the minuscule, educated, cosmopolitan elite, one nationalist newspaper concluded: 'If we desire the progress of our nation then we must give up our promenades on the paved streets of Istanbul. Let us go rather to the most remote corners of Kurdistan and establish printing presses' (p. 52).

Following the failure of the Sheikh Said and Ararat rebellions in the 1920s, the Bedir Khan brothers broke completely with their residual Turkish loyalties and sought to develop, with French support in Syria, a full-blown Kurdish nationalism. In *Les Massacres Kurdes en Turquie* and *The Case of Kurdistan against Turkey*, 'the Turks are portrayed as having pursued throughout the whole of their co-existence with the Kurds and other races the aims of extermination and assimilation [...] The Turks, descendants of Attila and Jingiz Khan, are an unchanging entity, barbaric and evil by nature' (p. 104). Although 'propagandistic in its simplistic, misleading, and distorted interpretations of Kurdish and Turkish history' (p. 111), 'Thurayya's [Bedir Khan's] publications had a tremendous influence on later writings on the Kurds [...] The statistics on deportations and losses contained in his booklets as well as his equally propagandist versions of historical events were integrated into many subsequent accounts of the Kurdish national struggle' (p. 114).

On the other hand, Strohmeier concludes that for 'the progress of Kurdish identity-building as manifested in nationalist writing, we must regard [Thurayya's] [...] publications as being of seminal importance' (pp. 100–1). In addition, Bedir Khan also cites the Turkish newspaper *Vakit* at length to illustrate 'that the Turkish government never regarded the Said Rebellion as essentially a religious revolt [as it always claimed] and was aware that the leaders had used religion as a screen' (p. 108) for their Kurdish nationalist purposes.

Strohmeier also analyses the writings of the Kurdish nationalist apostate or 'traitor' Shukru Mehmed Sekban. Using an allegory of three trees, Sekban 'crowns his argument for assimilation and the rejection of the entire concept of a separate Kurdish identity' (p. 122). This position, concludes Strohmeier, 'comprises an unusual documentation of the impingement of reality and failure on the [Kurdish] nationalist consciousness and of disillusionment' (p. 118). Sekban's metamorphosis might also have been a product of his wish to accept an amnesty and return to Turkey.

Part Three of Strohmeier' book deals with *Der Adler* [Eagle] *von Kurdistan*, a formalistic and forgotten attempt by Kamuran Bedir Khan to write a novel to project the Kurdish cause on the magnitude of Franz Werfel's classic *The Forty Days of Musa Dagh* for the Armenians. Strohmeier demonstrates how a close reading of this short book 'reveals a unique and fascinating attempt to fashion an image of Kurdishness incorporating the entire panoply of the imagined Kurdish nation and depicting their brave and just struggle for freedom [...]: their heroism, patriotism, reverence for their land, identification with their mountains; their pride in their language and heritage; the beauty of their folk tales and songs, the rich variety of their material culture; their strong and patriotic women; the solidarity among Kurds from all backgrounds' (p. 203). There is even an attempt to assert that the Kurds' 'true religion was Zoroastrianism' (p. 167) and that 'the legend of the Thousand Lakes [Bingol] is the Kurdish version of the biblical Garden of Eden' (p. 176).

Proverbs also constituted an important element of the Kurdish academic agenda: 'Lion, put your faith in your paws,' for example, indicated that 'the Kurds relied on their own strength and did not wait for divine assistance' (p. 190). Despite these early attempts to foster an onset of Kurdish nationalism, the more nationally conscious Sunni Arab majority led the way to the Franco-Syrian treaty of 1936 that resulted in Syrian independence as an Arab state immediately following the Second World War. It is to this situation that we now will turn.

Syrian independence

During the Second World War, the universal promises of the Atlantic Charter regarding national self-determination initially stirred Kurdish hopes. Although Jaladat Bedir Khan was in contact with foreign representatives in Damascus while his brother Kamuran acted as a quasi-Kurdish ambassador in Paris, the Kurds were unable to have their interests raised when the United Nations was created in 1945 because they lacked representation as a state. (Indeed it was not until April 1991 that the United Nations even mentioned the Kurds specifically, when, as a result of Saddam Hussein's defeat, it passed Security Council Resolution 688 which condemned 'the repression of the Iraqi civilian population [...] in Kurdish populated areas'.)

The first two decades of Syrian independence proved tumultuous as numerous military coups and attempts occurred. Two short-ruling military regimes in 1949 actually involved principals of Kurdish origin, Colonels Husni Zaim and Adib al-Shishakli, both of whom also had as their top aides men of similar ethnic roots, Muhsen Barazi and Fawzi Selo. However, neither Zaim or al-Shishakli emphasised his Kurdish background, spoke Kurdish or advocated Kurdish interests. Rather both were urban, Arabic-speakers who aroused little identification from the larger Kurdish population. Indeed, al-Shishakli proclaimed that Syria was a unified Arab-Muslim state, began the process of banning Kurdish organisations, dress and signs, and even argued that demands for minority privileges amounted to treason. Kurds began to be seen as hired agents for foreign enemies of Arab nationalism.

Egypt's staunchly Arab nationalist leader Gamal Abdul Nasser actually ruled a joint entity with Syria called the United Arab Republic from 1958 until 1961, but this period proved only a prelude to the assault against Kurdish interests that took place once Baathism came to power in the 1960s. As Jordi Tejel concluded, 'From the end of the 1950s, the Syrian army would experience several purges during which Kurdish officers were expelled from it, and the military academies and the police force both closed their doors to young Kurds.'[12]

The creation of the Kurdish Democratic Party in Syria (KDPS) in 1957—one of whose founders was Osman Sabri—also served as a pretext for strong measures against the Kurds. The KDPS simply asked for democracy in Syria and for the Kurds to be recognised as an ethnic group. The new party also pointed to the dearth of economic progress in the Kurdish areas of Syria and how Kurds were being discriminated against for positions in the police and military. In response, the government arrested Kurdish leaders and banned Kurdish publications. In addition, although the facts were never verified, the Kurds have always thought that the hostile government was responsible for a fire that killed 283 Kurdish children in a cinema in Amuda on 13 November 1960.[13] Thus, along with the Syrian Kurds' strategy of dissimulation or pretending to be part of the Syrian state,[14] the state's legal actions against the Kurds eventually contributed to their becoming virtually an invisible or forgotten people, the thesis of the following chapter.

2

THE FORGOTTEN

The situation regarding the Turkish origin of some of the Syrian Kurds described in Chapter 1 provided the Syrian government's rationale for the disenfranchisement of many of these Kurds in modern Syria. Never mind the fact that before the Sykes-Picot Agreement artificially separated the Kurds of the Ottoman Empire into three separate states after the First World War (Turkey, Iraq and Syria) all of these Kurds had lived within a single border.

Thus, following an exceptional census in 1962, Decree 93 classified some 120,000 Kurds, which at that time represented about 20 per cent of the Kurdish population in Syria, as *ajanib* who could not vote, own property or work in government jobs. They were issued red identity cards stating that they were not Syrian citizens. Their number has now risen to over 300,000 since the status of *ajanib* was inherited. Some 75,000 other Syrian Kurds were also known as *maktoumeen*. As such, they had virtually no civil rights and thus were even worse off than the *ajanib*. For a time they were able to get unofficial 'white papers' testifying to their identity from local authorities, but even this practice has now been discontinued. Their number has also grown over the years. 'The lack of nationality and identity documents means that stateless Kurds, for all practical purposes, are rendered non-existent. […] It is like being buried alive, said one man.'[1]

Given the arbitrary manner in which the Syrian government established these categories, siblings from the same family, born in the same Syrian village, could be listed differently. Fathers might be classified as *ajanib* while their children remained citizens. One man asserted, 'The grave of my grandfather is here in Syria; our family has been here for over 100 years, but we lost our nationality in 1962.'[2] Even such Kurdish notables as General Tawfiq Nizam al-Din, once the chief of staff of the Syrian army, were deprived of their Syrian citizenship and condemned to live in a legal vacuum. They were unable to travel legally domestically or abroad (which required a passport or domestic identification card), own property, enter into a legally recognised marriage, obtain food subsidies, and vote or hold elected or appointed office.

Although Kurdish children were supposed to possess the right to primary education—albeit not in their Kurdish mother tongue—statelessness made this very difficult for those seeking to enrol in secondary schools and universities. Those who managed still found it impossible to gain employment in their trained field. *Maktoumeen* children were not given diplomas from secondary schools, which prevented them from enrolling in a university. Thus, some took to using the names of relatives who did possess Syrian nationality to attend. A young man listed as a *maktoum* earned the highest grades in his class, but since he was not permitted to obtain a diploma upon graduation was unable to apply for entrance into a university.

Although *ajanib* can obtain a driver's licence and cash cheques, they are not allowed to have bank accounts or receive a commercial driver's licence. One *maktoum* man told how he received wages or signed contracts to work using the name of a friend who possessed Syrian nationality. Many others reported how companies exploited them because of their stateless situation. The public health service was also unavailable, which forced stateless Kurds to pay much higher costs for private services or, more likely, simply go without. More imaginative stateless Kurds used the identity cards of friends who still held citizenship.

Stateless Kurds who are married are considered single, which presents problems for their children and even prevents them from sharing a room in a hotel. Without nationality, Kurds are prohibited from owning property or registering a car or business. Again, some register using the names of friends or relatives, an arrangement that depends on the good faith of the legal person. Despite promises to solve these problems, little was done until the civil war that began in March 2011 forced the government to reassess its attitude toward the Kurds, a situation that will be considered in a later chapter.

The Baath party in power

After the nationalist, supposedly pan-Arab Baath party came to power in 1963,[3] the Arab nationalist plan to reduce the status of Kurds was furthered by the creation of an Arab Belt (*al-Hizam al-Arabi*) to expropriate the Kurds from their lands along the border with Turkey and Iraq and repopulate the area with 'loyal' Arabs. (In September 1956, the discovery of oil in the region [Qarachok and Remilan] also probably served as a motivation.) This Arab Belt was to be six to nine miles wide and extend some 170 miles along the Turkish border from Ras al-Ayn (Serekaniye in Kurdish) in Jazira province to the Iraqi border in the east. The dispossessed Kurds were forced either to leave Syria for Lebanon or to move into the Syrian interior. The evacuated Kurdish regions were then given Arab names in an effort to Arabise them and further the assimilation of any remaining Kurds who had already become deprived of education. The plan was only put into operation in 1973 because of technical problems, although further Arabisation was finally halted in 1976 but not reversed.

In 1967, school books began omitting the mention of Kurdish existence. A decree issued in 1977 further attempted to cleanse the Kurdish historic presence in Syria by providing for the dropping of non-Arabic place names. Thus, Kobani became Ain al-Arab, Serekaniye was changed to Ras al Ayn, while Derek became Al-Malikiyah. (Kurdish place names suffered even more in Turkey.) Two decrees in 1989 (1865/S/24 and 1865/S/24) prohibited the use of Kurdish in the workplace and during marriage ceremonies and festivities. Another government decree (No. 122) in September 1992 prohibited the registration of children with Kurdish first names, a policy that already had been implemented unofficially for many years. In May 2000, Resolution 768 provided that Kurdish cultural centres, bookshops and similar activities involving the selling of cassettes, videos and discs in the Kurdish language must also be banned. More recently, on 10 September 2008, Decree 49 amended Statute 41 of 26 October 2004 that had regulated the ownership, sale and lease of land in border regions. The Kurds saw this new decree as a tightening of the earlier Arab Belt policies that sought to dispossess them of their property.

Although these measures were not always enforced and bribes could sometimes help Kurds get around them, the mere existence of such regulations spoke to the state's hostility. Indeed, some have suspected that in return for giving the PKK of Turkey sanctuary in Syria for many years, the PKK kept the lid on Syrian Kurdish unrest. (This situation involving the PKK will be analysed in a later chapter.) As a result of all these legal provisions, little was heard about the Kurds in Syria compared with their co-nationals in other states of the Middle East. The Kurds in Syria, in effect, had become forgotten.

In addition, Articles 10, 11, 15 and 20 of the Baath party's constitution provided for an exclusive Arab nationalism that made any other political or even social groups not sharing this belief illegal. (Article I of the Syrian constitution mirrors these provisions by proclaiming: 'The people of the Syrian Arab Region are part of the Arab Nation, who work and struggle to achieve all-embracing unity.' In addition, Article 8 outlaws any other political party but the ruling Baathists and their coalition partners.) Although Michel Aflaq, one of the Baath party founders, who was ironically a Christian, recognised that there were ethnic minorities within the Arab nation, he argued that the Kurds would want to remain within the Arab purview because being part of such a vast nation would ensure their welfare. Thus, the Kurds might be tolerated as long as they accepted the Baathist concept of Arab nationalism.

In practice, however, the Baathists came to view the Kurds as a foreign group that was a menace to the Arab nation. Even more, of course, after he came to power in November 1970, Hafez al-Assad reduced the supposedly pan-Arab Baath party to a mere façade for his own Alawite family's personal property. Thus, as mentioned above and as a result of all these legal provisions and political initiatives, the Kurds in Syria, in effect, had become forgotten.

M. Talab Hilal manuscript

The theoretical justification for these harsh, discriminatory measures was a clandestine treatise written and then published by Lieutenant Muhammad Talab Hilal, the chief of the Syrian security police in the province of Hasaka (Jazira), on 12 November 1963. The title of his manual translated into English as *National, Political, and Social Study of the Province of Jazira*. A look at some of this book's main points would be very enlightening as to why many Kurds in Syria feel alienated towards that state.[4]

- The bells of alarm in Jazira call on Arab conscience to save this region, purify it and rid it of the dirt and historical refuse [the Kurds] of history in order to preserve the riches of this Arab territory (p. 2).
- People such as the Kurds—who have no history, civilisation, language, or ethnic origin—are prone to committing violence and destruction as are all mountain people (pp. 4–5).
- The Kurdish question advanced by them has become a malignant tumour on the side of the Arab nation and must be removed (p. 6).
- They [the Kurds] are supported by the imperialists since the goals of these Middle East outlaws are similar to their goals (p. 12).
- The imperialists are trying to legitimise the Kurdish question as they legitimised that of the state of Israel (p. 14).
- The Kurdish question is the most dangerous threat to the Arab nation, especially Jazira and northern Iraq. It is evolving as the Zionist movement did before Israel was established. The Jazira Kurds tried to prevent the Syrian army from intervening on behalf of the Arab state of Iraq against [Mulla Mustafa] Barzani (p. 24).
- The Kurds of Turkey live north of the Kurdish belt of Syria. The Kurds of both countries are blood brothers and many of their tribes are spread all over Turkey, Syria, and Iraq. They are ready on horsebacks at the frontiers for the realisation of their golden dream of the Kurdish homeland, Kurdistan (pp. 24–6).
- Despite their differences, the Jazira Kurdish tribes are united and inspired by one idea, which is the Kurdish race. This one desire has given them the strength to pursue their national dream of a Kurdish homeland (pp. 26–8).
- The Kurds differ from the Arabs ethnically, psychologically, and physiologically.
- Though they do not speak an acceptable form of Arabic, the majority of the Muslim *ulamas* [religious leaders] in the Hasaka province are Kurds; they are conspiring to create their nation under the guise of religion (pp. 38–40).

To excise this threat of what he termed 'a malignant tumour on the side of the Arab nation', Muhammed Talab Hilal recommended the creation of an Arab Belt—extending some 200 miles along the Syrian-Turkish border and having a depth of six to nine miles—in which all Kurds would be removed and replaced by Arab settlers. The Kurds would have their lands confiscated, be stripped of their citizenship, have their employment opportunities restricted and be denied public social services, medical treatment and schooling. Further justification for such drastic action included the ignorant claim that the Kurds 'have no history, civilization, language, or ethnic origin', while also representing a threat to the Arab nation analogous to that of the Zionist movement in Israel.

Although it is correct that many (but not all) Kurds do dream of an independent Kurdistan and, as already noted above, some came to Syria from Turkey after the failed uprisings of the 1920s, the Hilal treatise ignores the fact that, as mentioned above, the borders between Turkey and Syria that now divided the Kurds were only established following the First World War and thus artificially separated the Kurds, just as many Arab nationalists have argued they also artificially separated the Arabs. In truth, Kurdish and Arab tribes had contested the Hasaka region for hundreds of years, and around the beginning of the twentieth century this struggle had climaxed in a bitter conflict between Ibrahim Pasha's Kurdish Milli confederation and the powerful Arab Shammar tribe. After their arrival, the then French authorities favoured the Kurds as a way to strengthen their claims to the area. Indeed, the Terrier Plan (named after Captain Pierre Terrier) was a French proposal in the 1920s to encourage the Kurdish nationalists to concentrate their political ambitions only on Jazira (Hasaka) province and not seek to tie this with other Kurdish enclaves in Mandatory Syria.[5] In addition, the French also allowed the pan-Kurdish nationalist party, Khoybun (Independence), to operate out of Syria for several years after its creation in 1927.[6]

Even more, of course, the Kurds who had come from Turkey and were now living in Syria had been living there since the 1920s when they had been issued identity cards by the then French authorities. Thus, these Kurds were already Syrian citizens when that state became independent in 1946. Stripping them of their citizenship was a clear violation of international law regarding nationality rights in cases of state succession as well as such international and legally binding human-rights doctrines as the Universal Declaration of Human Rights, the International Covenant on Civil and Political Rights, the Convention on the Rights of the Child and the International Convention on the Elimination of All Forms of Racial Discrimination.[7]

Kurdish political parties

Ironically, one might argue that the weak and fractured Kurdish political party system in Syria is another reason why the Kurds in that state were forgotten until the civil war led to their sudden emergence in July 2012. Although Khoybun, created in 1927 as a transnational Kurdish party, had lingered on until 1944, its main target had been Turkey from where many of its members had originally come. In addition, Khoybun had focused its attention on France and Syrian nationalists, and did not see itself as a Kurdish party in Syria with a Kurdish nationalist agenda that focused mainly on Syria. Its short-lived successor, the Kurdish League (1945–46) continued this position so as not to antagonise the authorities in Damascus.

Ironically, so many Syrian Kurds were involved with the Syrian Communist Party (SCP) during the 1930s and 1940s—seeing communism as their best strategy against Arab nationalism—that it was called the 'Kurdish Party'.[8] Its leader, Khalid Bakdash, was a Kurd from Hayy al-Akrad or the Kurdish quarter in Damascus. Although some saw Bakdash as an example of an Arabised Kurd, he maintained social and political relations with Kurdish nationalists like Rewshen Bedir Khan, the widow of Jaladet Bedir Khan, and was also able to speak Kurdish.

Thus, it was not until 14 June 1957 that the first modern Kurdish political party was formed, the Kurdish Democratic Party in Syria (KDPS). Even so, the KDPS maintained a Syrian national agenda that did not call for the liberation of a Syrian Kurdistan. Rather, it was concerned with the improvement of Kurdish socio-economic conditions. Indeed, it is revealing that none of the numerous Kurdish parties currently use the sensitive term Kurdistan in their names, for fear that it might incite government fears of secession. Such concerns have never troubled the Kurdish parties in Turkey, Iraq or Iran.

Nevertheless, it was the growth of a chauvinistic Arab nationalism as well as the conclusion that Kurdish rights would not be protected by the SCP that helped lead to the KDPS' formation. The previously mentioned Osman Sabri is often listed as the founder of the KDPS, although in truth this title should be shared with a number of others who in time were to split the party. The young Jalal Talabani, who often found refugee in Damascus during those days, also played an important role in the party's creation as the Syrian Kurds were closely following the develop-

25

ment of Kurdish nationalism in neighbouring Iraq and were thus clearly influenced by such transnational events. Indeed the KDPS served as a propaganda outlet for the Kurdistan Democratic Party (KDP) in Iraq, to which Talabani still belonged and whose then leader, Mulla Mustafa Barzani, he then greatly admired and served.

Despite this pedigree of Kurdish nationalism, Syrian political parties have never taken up arms against the government as have Kurdish parties in Iraq, Turkey and Iran. Indeed, even during the Syrian civil war that began in 2011, the myriad of Kurdish parties hesitated to join the opposition and preferred to follow a third or middle road between the government and the opposition, as will be analysed in a later chapter. The main reason for this strategic line was probably their greater perceived weakness compared with their regional kin and the lack of any accessible mountains to serve as a sanctuary.[9]

Whether because of, or in spite of, the Kurdish hesitancy to take it on directly, the Syrian government, newly split from Nasser's UAR and determined to maintain and build its Arab identity, renamed the state the Syrian *Arab* Republic (emphasis added) and accused the Syrian Kurds of supporting Barzani's Kurdish uprising in neighbouring Iraq. Osman Sabri and Nureddin Zaza were among thirty-two leading members of the KDPS arrested in September 1962. These arrests helped Hamid Haj Darwish, a young law student, become the new leader. He too was arrested in 1965, but released after ten months. Other Kurds accused him of collusion with the government, a petard that has become common among the Syrian Kurdish parties.

Splits in the KDPS occurred in 1965 and again, to a greater extent, in 1970 between supporters of Osman Sabri on the one hand, and Hamid Darwish and Nureddin Zaza on the other. Sabri wanted to continue a stronger struggle for Kurdish rights, while Darwish and Zaza argued for a softer approach. Sabri's faction kept the name Kurdish Democratic Party in Syria and became known as *el-Parti* (the Party), while Darwish's faction took the name Kurdish Democratic Progressive Party in Syria. Sabri's leftist faction consisted of teachers, students and former communists, while Darwish's rightist group contained notables such as urban merchants, professionals, religious leaders and landowners. On the transnational/regional level, the former sided with Barzani's then-perceived more militant group, while the later identified with Talabani, then seen as more accommodating. The latter would later form his own Iraqi

Kurdish party, the Patriotic Union of Kurdistan (PUK), which he formally declared in Damascus on 1 June 1975 after Barzani's defeat in his war against Baghdad.

Over the years a host of small political parties emerged, with more than ten now claiming to be heirs to the original KDPS and maybe another five also in existence, each division and new nomenclature adding to the confusion and party transience. Indeed there are even two completely separate parties using exactly the same name. Several different coalitions also exist, but with the outbreak of the Syrian civil war in 2011, it was clear that the PKK-affiliated Democratic Union Party (PYD)— only created in 2003—had suddenly emerged as by far the strongest, while the bewildering array of others loosely constituted the so-called Kurdish National Coalition (KNC).

This perplexing disunity was caused by links to different Kurdish parties outside of Syria as well as personal and traditional ties of loyalty to families and tribes. Although tactical differences were usually more important, ideological differences over such issues as the nature and scale of political activity have also contributed to this divisive milieu. Moderate/rightists favoured dialogue with the government, while leftists were more inclined to favour demonstrations and similar activist approaches.[10] In addition, Jordi Tejel argues that the government's policy of selective/ partial alliance or 'collusive transactions' with some parties have alienated and split them from others.[11]

The situation was all the more damning for the Syrian parties because the new kingpin PYD was not fully even a Syrian entity given its PKK roots. All of this will be analysed in greater detail in a later chapter, but at this point it should simply be reiterated that the fractured, transient and even obscure nature of the Syrian political parties[12] (with the exception of today's PYD) contributed to what, until the Syrian civil war broke out, was the forgotten character of the Kurds in Syria.

3

WOMEN

Although it is arguably true that women have been abused and degraded in modern Western society by pornography, immodest attire and sexual discrimination in general, it is perhaps also true that the West might be considered far more advanced than the Islamic world in modern times in its earlier implementation of women's rights. As long as women—half the population or more—are not treated equally with men it is not possible for a society to advance. Therefore, to fully understand why the Kurds in Syria were largely forgotten, we must examine what the situation for women there was and still is.

First of all, however, it should be granted that most observers have long commented on how women have fared somewhat better in Kurdish society than they do elsewhere in much of the Middle East. True, as in most traditional and Islamic societies, men are given certain rights and responsibilities in Kurdish society that are denied to women. Given the differences dictated by biology, men are supposed to govern, fight and support their families, while women are supposed to bear and care for children, manage their households and obey their husbands.

Nevertheless, by comparison with the other Islamic societies around them, Kurdish women have often exercised more freedom. Indeed, travellers have long noted how Kurdish women usually went unveiled and were allowed greater freedom, while also performing most of the hard manual labour. Even in marriage, Kurdish women could sometimes be wooed and won, although arranged marriages also existed. Wives too were treated more as equals by their husbands than they were in most other Middle Eastern locales. Kurdish women have also held a more secure financial position than women in some other Middle Eastern societies. Women, for example, could more easily succeed their husbands as the head of a family even when there were male children.

Kurdish women have also occasionally played prominent roles in politics and the military.[1] Lady Kara Fatima of Marash won fame as a female warrior who led hundreds of Kurds against the Russians in the Russo-Turkish War of 1877 and represented the Kurds in the Ottoman court in Constantinople. The last autonomous ruler of the Hakkari region was a woman. Adela Khanum was a famous and cultured chief of the Jaf tribe until her death in 1924. Although actually an Assyrian, Margaret George was a more recent example of a Kurdish female warrior. Hero Talabani, the wife of Jalal Talabani, is a well-known personality in her own right. More than 30 per cent of the parliament of the KRG elected on 25 July 2009 is female. Leyla Zana, a female Kurdish politician from Turkey, is famous for her advocacy of Kurdish human rights. Both the PKK and PYD have set themselves apart from other groups in the Middle East including Kurdish ones by emphasising women's rights. Indeed, many women have famously joined and fought in the ranks of the PKK and PYD militants. In addition, the *Asayesh* or PYD police/security forces also include women.

As of August 2013, the PYD in Syria is co-chaired by both a male (Salih Muslim) and a female (Asia Abdullah), as is the pro-Kurdish Peace and Democracy Party (BDP) in Turkey, whose male co-chair is Selahattin Dermirtas while its female co-chair is Gultan Kisanak. In addition, the BDP maintains a gender quota of 40 per cent throughout its structure. Finally, many have argued that if women had not taught their children to speak Kurdish before they had to learn Turkish or Arabic in school or at work, the Kurdish language would have perished by now. Instead it managed to survive and, given recent Kurdish advances discussed in this book, is being modernised and more fully institutionalised. Indeed, accordingly to linguists, Kurdish is approximately the fortieth in numerical strength among the several thousand languages spoken around the world today.[2]

Despite these examples, women's rights, or the lack thereof, are increasingly issues in Kurdistan. For example, even the PKK remains largely a male-dominated organisation, especially at its higher levels. KAMER, the independent Kurdish women's group referred to below, has come under pressure from the PKK, which wants to control such organisations. Asia Abdullah, seems to be only a token when one considers the much more prominent role played by her male counterpart Salih Muslim. Indeed, arguably the most comprehensive and recent scholarly study of the situation dismisses the Western and Kurdish nationalist romanticism of the women of Kurdistan and instead offers a complex portrait of their oppression and resistance.[3] Kurdish women in Turkey, for example, have sometimes been subjected to various forms of state violence including rape and sexual harassment, especially during the years of violence associated with the insurgency between the government and the PKK in the 1980s and 1990s.

On the other hand, this conflict led Kurdish women to develop a new consciousness that questioned the prevalent sexism of both the government and Kurdish men and led to an organised political activism.[4] KAMER, a women's non-governmental organisation established in Diyarbakir in 1997, now has branches in twenty-three provinces and is operating in eighteen more.[5] These women tell how the PKK conflict forced them into urban areas where they were barely able to exist, a situation that then led to frustration and increased domestic violence. Many women also had to care for themselves and their children because their husbands and male relatives had been killed or imprisoned.

Nearly half the Kurdish women surveyed by KAMER were younger than eighteen when married. Seventy per cent had been forced into arranged marriages, the vast majority to relatives. *Berdel* (the traditional custom of two families exchanging brides) still applied to almost 5 per cent of the women. Supposed suicides were sometimes probably honour killings (see below) made to look like suicides, or women forced into killing themselves.

On the other hand, more recently there have been 'changing gender relations'[6] in Turkey. Regarding marriages, for example, 'It seems that most families today are more concerned about their children's, particularly their daughter's, preferences than in the past.'[7] *Besik kertmesi* (the traditional custom of being promised in marriage while still an infant) has declined to less than 0.5 per cent. *Kuma* (second wives) marriage has also been decreasing. In addition, 'there is [...] marked contrast in the way women with different education levels are treated'.[8] Since 1995, the 'Saturday Mothers' have been protesting every Saturday in front of the Galatasaray Lycee in Istanbul, demanding to know what happened to their relatives who disappeared after being taken into state custody.

The KRG in northern Iraq has recently sought to deal with honour killing, the murder of women—usually by their own male family members—because the women are deemed to have violated traditional codes of sexual mores and thus to have dishonoured the family. Men frequently commit honour killing as a tool of repression against women. Until recently, the courts largely tolerated it, but recently honour killing has become an important issue in women's and human rights.

Female genital mutilation (FGM) or female circumcision is the intentional partial removal of the clitoris, practised for traditional cultural and religious reasons in the Middle East and elsewhere, including the Kurdish areas. Advocates argue that it reduces the sexual desire of women and thus makes them eligible for marriage and less likely to be unfaithful to their husbands. Critics correctly dismiss such ignorant claims and point out that the practice can lead to long-term health problems, including infection, painful sexual intercourse, psychological trauma and sterility. The problem is particularly prevalent among many Kurdish women, even in the diaspora. In recent years, there has been an attempt to end FGM, but the practice continues because of its sensitive nature and its frequent association with conservative cultural and religious beliefs. The most recent (2012) US State Department annual Country Report on Syria asserted that most reports of FGM in Syria are 'primarily in rural Kurdish communities'.

Female Kurdish refugees and widows suffer more than their male counterparts.[9] During the genocidal Anfal campaign waged against the Iraqi Kurds by Baghdad in 1989, as many as 180,000 Kurds were killed. Women who were arrested and detained in camps faced particularly harrowing situations. In one particularly humiliating experience, 'The [Iraqi] soldiers put a woman's undergarment on a stick and raised it in the air. "*Hay allam Akrad*," they shouted: "This is the Kurdish flag."'[10] In general, much clearly remains to be done regarding women's rights in Kurdistan.

In Syria particularly, as noted above, many of the regime's agrarian reforms discriminated against the Kurds who were denied full rights to property, citizenship, loans, state employment and benefits, and access to health systems and education, and thus relegated Kurds even more deeply into poverty.[11] Kurdish women suffered even more because they suddenly faced increased responsibilities, as well as discrimination in water distribution and property rights, owing to male migration away from rural areas in search of profitable employment. In a village close to al-Bab, east of Aleppo, eight out of every ten men migrated to cities to find work. The resulting impact on the workload of women proved crushing. Rural women suffered more than urban ones, as illustrated by the Euphrates Basin Development Project—which was supposed to initiate agricultural reforms, irrigation, damming and pilot farms aimed at increasing agricultural production and food security in the fertile Jazira province during the 1960s, but excluded the Kurds.

In this situation, many Kurdish women in Syria have been forced to work also as wage labourers to provide for their families. The lack of protective labour laws led to women and young children being exploited as cheap agricultural wage workers. Women received only 75 per cent of the money that male labourers did and thus at times had to enter into unwanted relationships with men just to survive. In addition, women agricultural workers were not entitled to land and water access rights and so usually had to rely on their husbands to acquire seeds and other agricultural products, which were sold only to the person officially holding title to the land. Even more, women were not allowed to sell agricultural products, a right reserved only to men. This state of affairs put women in a disempowered position of legal and economic dependency made all the more difficult because women faced discrimination regarding water distribution.

Furthermore, many Kurdish families in Syria could not afford to have more than one child placed in a school, a position usually given to the son. Even if they managed to enter school, many girls dropped out to help their families take care of younger children, carry water and perform chores in the household. This lack of education reduced the girls' options and often led to unfortunate marriages at an early age. Given all these factors, 'Syrian Kurdish women suffered doubly, through state […] and gender discrimination,'[12] a situation that has been referred to as the 'feminisation of poverty [and] the creation of an exploited female proletariat'.[13] To urge the elimination of all forms of discrimination against Kurdish women and promote their participation in the social, political, economic and educational spheres of life irrespective of their religious, political or other beliefs, the Kurdish Human Rights Project in London drew up *The Charter for the Rights and Freedoms of Women in the Kurdish Regions and Diaspora*.[14] Although it constitutes only soft law or aspirations for the future, this Charter represents a modern standard for a better world of gender relationships among the Kurds.

4

TRANSNATIONAL ACTORS

Referring to what he termed 'the incontestable reality of the transborder character of the Kurdish question', one knowledgeable observer then elaborated on 'the understanding, on the part of the Syrian Kurds, that the border was more a common space, in terms of language, tribal affiliation, ethnicity, and family, than a line of separation'.[1] Thus, for example, what the existing states call illegal smuggling across international borders can be for the Kurds simply intra-Kurdish commerce. Clearly, given the lack of their own state and dispersal over four Middle Eastern states as well a considerable diaspora in Europe, the Kurds inevitably engage in and are affected by transnational actors, both state and non-state. States such as Turkey, Iraq, Lebanon, Iran, Israel, the United States and Russia, among others, and non-states such as the PKK, the KRG in Iraq—including even more its two main political parties the KDP and PUK—and the European Union (EU), among others, are all examples. Thus, it is important to analyse interactions between the Kurds in Syria with those in other states and various non-state organisations. How did each affect and view each other? How important have these transnational relations been for the Kurds in Syria?

States

Turkey

Founded as an ethnic Turkish state upon the ruins of the multinational Ottoman Empire following the First World War, until recently Turkey

35

has taken an almost schizophrenic attitude towards the Kurds, fearing that their national claims would potentially destroy Turkish territorial integrity. Indeed, during the 1920s and 1930s, Turkey crushed three great Kurdish uprisings: Sheikh Said in 1925, Ararat in 1930 and Dersim (now called Tunceli) in 1938. All Kurdish schools, organisations and publications, and religious institutions such as *tekiyes* (Sufi fraternities) and *madrasahs* (religious schools) were closed. The name 'Mountain Turks' when referring to the Kurds in Turkey served as a code term for these actions and the refusal to even recognise the existence of the Kurds.

Naturally Turkey also closely monitored Kurdish activities over the borders. Khoybun's backing from its political base in Syria of the Ararat rebellion from 1927 to 1930 illustrated that this fear of the Kurds was not entirely misplaced. Although both conventions were supposedly fashioned to contain Soviet expansion while also acting as non-aggression pacts, the Treaty of Saadabad in 1937 and subsequently the Baghdad Pact (formally known as the Middle East Treaty Organisation) in 1955 implicitly obligated Turkey, Iran and Iraq to co-operate on the Kurdish issue. This collaboration included measures to prevent cross-border communication and support among the Kurds and, in general, sought to prevent any joint, transnational Kurdish action that might challenge the current international boundaries set up following the First World War. Syria was certainly a silent partner in both endeavours, and therefore its Kurds were silent victims.

In August 1944 Mount Dalanpur, located where Turkey, Iraq and Iran converge, was the site of a famous meeting of Kurdish delegates from those three states as well as Syria. The participants signed a treaty known as *Peyamiani sei Sanowar* (The Treaty of the Three Boundaries) in which they pledged mutual support, the sharing of resources, and the restoration of the Kurdish language and culture. Although this meeting did not result in any practical Kurdish unity, it did illustrate the existence of transnational Kurdish aspirations and thus, correspondingly, threats to the states in which Kurds lived at this early date. For example, the failed Mahabad Republic of Kurdistan in Iran in 1946 under its revered leader Qazi Muhammad still resonates in the development of transnational Kurdish nationalism including among the Kurds in Syria. As of December 2013, another scheduled pan-Kurdish conference in Irbil had still not taken place. Given the Kurds' growing empowerment, it will be interesting to see what its transnational results will be.

Over the years, Turkey has even had occasion to intervene militarily many times into northern Iraq because of the Kurdish situation. Indeed, it was not until 1926 that Turkey finally conceded northern Iraq or Mosul, the name used to refer to the *vilayet* (province) in Ottoman times, to Iraq. Subsequently, in unsuccessful attempts to root out the PKK sanctuaries in northern Iraq, Turkey has intervened militarily on numerous occasions and as recently as 2011. It is only recently that Turkey has come to see the possibilities of co-operation with the KRG and even began formal negotiations with the PKK in January 2013. As will be shown below, these initiatives have already had important effects on the Kurds in Syria by leading Turkey to take a somewhat less hostile attitude towards the PKK-affiliated PYD.

Indeed, Ankara has played a key role in assisting the opposition in the Syrian civil war. The Syrian National Council (before it was succeeded by the Syrian National Coalition in November 2012) was founded and largely based in Istanbul, while the opposition Free Syrian Army (FSA) maintains its nominal headquarters in south-eastern Turkey. However, in indiscriminately supporting the FSA, Turkey also has been aiding Jabhat al-Nursa and the Islamic State of Iraq and Syria (ISIS), armed groups affiliated with al-Qaeda that are part of the Syrian opposition, but opposed to the Syrian Kurds.

On the other hand, the PYD founded in Syria in 2003 by the PKK has been enjoying *de facto* autonomy just across the border from Turkey since 19 July 2012 when the increasingly beleaguered Assad regime pulled most of its troops out of the Kurdish areas in order to concentrate on maintaining its position in the centre and west of the country. Although it might be one latent reason why Turkey decided to open negotiations with the PKK in 2013, the resulting situation in Syria has played havoc in Turkey. However, if Turkey intervenes against the PYD, it risks getting bogged down in a quagmire. In addition, the al-Qaeda-affiliated groups mentioned above that are supported by Turkey have already fallen into conflict with the PYD. Indeed, in March 2012, Murat Karayilan, the PKK military leader holed up in his Qandil mountains sanctuary on the Iraqi-Iranian border, declared that, 'If the Turkish state intervenes against our people in Western Kurdistan, all of Kurdistan will turn into a war zone.'[2] Nevertheless, the PYD has already clashed on numerous occasions with the Turkish-backed al-Qaeda militants referred to above in Kurdish-populated areas of Syria.[3]

In July 2013, these battles intensified as Turkish policy towards Syria and the PYD lurched towards crisis.[4] Fearing the effect on its own disaffected Kurds, Turkey has also repeatedly warned the Syrian Kurds, who have raised the PYD flag only fifty metres from the Turkish border, not to declare autonomy.[5] Turkey's foreign minister Ahmet Davutoglu declared that, 'we expect three basic things from the Kurds in Syria. […] Firstly for them not to co-operate with the regime. […] The second is for them not to form a de-facto foundation based on ethnic or religious bases. […] The third is for them not to engage in activities that could endanger the security of the Turkish border.'[6]

In a surprise visit to Istanbul on 26 July 2013, Salih Muslim, the leader of the PYD, assured the Turkish authorities that the Syrian Kurds continued to see themselves as part of Syria and posed no threat to Turkey's territorial integrity. However, he did add that the Kurds in Syria needed to establish 'a temporary serving administration till the chaos in Syria is over'.[7]

Others

During the days of the French mandate (1920–46), France of course played an important role. Among many French actors, two noted scholars of Kurdish studies, Pierre Rondot and Roger Lescot, also gave covert aid to the Kurds, working specifically with the Bedir Khan brothers. For their part, 'the leaders of the Kurdish nationalist movement showed themselves ready to collaborate with the French orientalists in order to create a wave of sympathy, or Kurdophilia, among the high ranks of French diplomacy and also among the French public'.[8] Using his 'longstanding Zionist undercover connections',[9] Kamuran Bedir Khan worked with Israeli intelligence during the first Arab-Israeli War in 1948, arguing that Israel should support minorities like the Kurds to overthrow the Syrian government and encourage Kurdish national aspirations throughout the region. This, of course, was an aspect of the old Zionist idea of creating 'mosaic States' that would favour the minorities within the boundaries of Arab states.

In the early years of the Second World War, Kamuran Bedir Khan was also behind Radio Levant's thirty-minute radio broadcasts twice a week from Beirut to Turkey. In addition, he read the news in Kurmanji Kurdish,[10] a powerful symbol of lingering Kurdish nationalism in Syria and Turkey despite Khoybun's ultimate failure. Indeed, in 1928, Kamuran's elder brother Thurayya (Sureya) had even journeyed to Detroit in the United States in an attempt to interest the Kurdish community living there in supporting the Ararat rebellion.[11] This situation illustrates that the Arab majority was not always simply paranoid about the minorities existing within their states. Jordi Tejel even argues that the Syrian government issued the notorious Decree 93 that stripped 20 per cent of the Kurds in Syria of their citizenship in 1962 in part because of transnational influences involving the minority Kurds: 'The regional context is of great importance for this particular issue. The year 1962 was one of significant progress for the Iraqi Kurds who held all of the north of Kurdistan.'[12]

In its heyday and even into the Second World War era, Khoybun entered into secret diplomatic relations with agents from numerous other states including the United States, Britain, Germany, Italy and the Soviet Union.[13] During the 1940s and early 1950s—when given the lack of any Kurdish nationalist parties, most politically active Kurds in Syria belonged to the Syrian Communist Party—radio broadcasts from Yerevan in Soviet Armenia spread the message that the Soviet Union represented the best hope for achieving Kurdish nationalist goals.

More recently, of course, Syrian Kurdish exile groups such as the Reform Party of Syria led by Farid Ghadri in the United States and the Western Kurdistan Association led by Jawad Mella in Britain, among others, have operated transnationally. In addition Syrian Kurdish conferences also were held in Paris in December 2005, Washington in March 2006 and Brussels in May 2006. The aim of the third conference was to unify all the Kurdish political parties operating in Syria and abroad as well as independents. The United States helped create and support this latter conference, but despite initial commitments, most of the participants backed out. Fear that they would not be possible to control an exclusively exile group and reluctance to be viewed as American pawns probably explain this failure.

To the extent that their intervention in the Syrian civil war also impacts the Kurds in Syria, the United States, Russia, Iran, Saudi Arabia, Qatar, Britain, France, Iraq, Lebanon, Jordan and Israel, among others, including of course the EU, are also involved transnational state actors today. Lebanon and Israel, two states earlier described as not yet involved but possessing byways into Syria's final denouement, are actually now already involved. Lebanon has had a Shiite district in south Beirut and two Sunni mosques in Tripoli bombed. Israel would certainly like to see the end of Assad, but his replacement could be even more hostile to the Jewish state. Better to keep the devil you at least know. Finally the United States' role will merit an entire subsequent chapter.

Non-State Actors

The PKK

The PYD illustrates the importance of examining transnational actors as it owes its very existence to the PKK in 2003. And of course the PKK was formally created in Turkey in November 1978, headquartered in Syria from 1979 to 1998 and then moved to the Qandil Mountains on the north-eastern Iraqi border with Iran, where it still finds sanctuary while also being active throughout a large Kurdish diaspora, particularly in Europe. Thus, to understand today's most important Syrian Kurdish political party, as already stated, one must study a variety of inter-related transnational actors, both state and non-state.

Beginning in May 1979, the Assad regime gave the PKK what might be termed a strategic alliance when its long-time leader Abdullah Ocalan, sensing the military coup that was to occur in Turkey in September 1980, first arrived.[14] There are several reasons for this situation but water was probably the main one as Turkey controlled the flow of the Euphrates River into Syria. As Turkey's Guneydogu Anadolu Projesi (GAP) or Southeast Anatolia Project, of harnessing the rivers to the north, neared completion, Syria began to use the PKK as a bargaining tool in an unsuccessful attempt to obtain a more favourable guaranteed annual water quota from Turkey. Smouldering animosities regarding the Turkish annexation of Alexandretta (in Turkish, Hatay) in the closing days of the French mandate, also contributed to Syria's support for the PKK. Indeed, to this day Syrian maps still show the province as part of Syria. (Damascus feels the same way about Lebanon, which was prised loose from Syria by the French to administer their mandates more successfully.)

Many also argue that Syria gave the PKK sanctuary in return for it keeping the lid on Syria's Kurds. Thus Hafez al-Assad allowed Syrian Kurds to join the PKK in lieu of serving in the Syrian army. One estimate suggested that from 7,000 to 10,000 Syrian Kurds were killed in clashes between the Turkish army and the PKK.[15] Indeed Ocalan went so far as to declare publicly in 1996 that most of the Kurds in Syria were refugees from Turkey and thus not Syrian.[16] The PKK leader rationalised this cynical position as being merely a temporary, tactical one necessary to pursue the more important struggle against Turkey.

Although some might argue that this tactic would have sown mistrust and even disdain for the PKK among the Kurds of Syria, in the long run it did not, as is illustrated by the eventual rise of the PYD. The PKK's armed struggle for an independent pan-Kurdish state fostered sympathy and hope for tangible results, in contrast to the other Syrian parties which avoided conflict and seemed almost invisible in comparison. Even though the Kurds in Syria avoided armed struggle, the revolts in Turkey of Sheikh Said in 1925, and Ararat in 1927, and in Iraq of Barzani as recently as 1975, were staples of the Kurdish national narrative in Syria. Indeed, even before the advent of the PKK, Syrian Kurds had joined Kurdish guerrilla movements in neighbouring northern Iraq. Other factors helping to explain the PKK's growth included 'a feeling of national solidarity, getting away from the social control of the elders, for women, freedom from the patriarchy, [and] individual interests (access to material and symbolic resources)'.[17]

Thus, for almost two decades the PKK was sheltered and permitted to grow in Syria. Ocalan commuted between an apartment in Damascus and various PKK bases in the countryside. For many years the Mazlum (Mahsun) Korkmaz camp in the Syrian-controlled Bekaa Valley in Lebanon was the most important one until Assad closed it down as a sop to the Turks in 1992. Other camps appeared, however, one being very close to Damascus; the present author visited there in March 1998. This site contained several buildings, housed hundreds of guerrillas and even possessed recreational facilities.

However, the dialogue of the deaf between Turkey and Syria over this issue finally came to an end in October 1998 when Turkey threatened to go to war unless Syria expelled the PKK. Under the Adana Agreement, the PKK was shut down in Syria, while Ocalan and most of his guerrillas were expelled. Ocalan was then captured in Kenya by a joint US-Turkish operation on 15 February 1999. At first the PKK leader was sentenced to death, but this fate was changed to a life prison term on the island of Imrali off the coast of Istanbul where the PKK leader remains incarcerated to this day. Some PKK members were imprisoned in Syria, while a few others were handed over to Turkey, but the vast majority of the actual guerrillas left for the Qandil mountains in Iraq.

After almost two decades of activity based in Syria, however, a potential base remained among the sympathetic population. In October 2003, the PKK in effect reincarnated its Syria branch under the new name Democratic Union Party (PYD), leaving out the term Kurdistan or even Kurdish, nomenclature that might have been chosen to appease the Syrian authorities. Fuat Omar became the new leader. According to one analysis the newly reformed PKK-affiliate played 'the central role'[18] in the *Serhildan* or Qamishli riots of March 2004, arguably the formative event for the sudden current Syrian Kurdish awareness that will be analysed in a subsequent chapter.

Omar was succeeded by Salih Muslim (Mohammed) in 2010. Imprisoned by the Syrian authorities for a while, Muslim was eventually released and withdrew to a PKK camp in the Qandil mountains of northern Iraq from where the authorities allowed him to return to Syria in April 2011, just as the civil war was beginning. (This return reminds one of Lenin's secret return to Russia in 1917.)

Although the PYD denies any organic links to the PKK, the connection is illustrated institutionally by the PYD being one of the constituent members of the *Koma Civaken Kurdistan* (KCK) or Kurdistan Communities Union, an umbrella organisation created by the PKK around 2005 that supposedly unites the PKK with a host of other Kurdish organisations including those in Turkey, Iran, Iraq and Europe. Moreover, in his study of Syria's Kurds, Jordi Tejel refers to the PYD as the 'ex-PKK' on at least two occasions.[19]

Further illustrating the PKK/Syria connection, one study found that as of 2007, 20 per cent of the PKK's troops stationed in the Qandil mountains were of Syrian origin,[20] while, at the same time, Fehman Huseyin (Dr Bahoz Erdal, his *nom de guerre* in reference to being a dentist) is a Syrian Kurd who commanded the *Hezen Parastina Gel* (HPG) or Peoples Defence Force, the PKK's military arm. Subsequently, however, the hardline Huseyin was succeeded by Murat Karayilan, a Kurd from Turkey who was supposedly more moderate. Salih Muslim, the leader of the PYD, also said that his party had discussed the first draft of a proposed interim government for the Syrian Kurds with the PKK as well as the two main Iraqi Kurdish parties, the Kurdistan Democratic Party (KDP) and the Patriotic Union of Kurdistan (PUK).[21]

The Iraqi Kurds[22]

First as political parties (the KDP and PUK), but also since its creation in 1992 and constitutional recognition in 2003 as the KRG, the Iraqi Kurds have played a crucial role as transnational actors interacting with and influencing the Syrian Kurds. As Mishaal Tammo, the leader of the Kurdish Future Movement (Party) in Syria, explained, 'The Iraqi war liberated us from a culture of fear. […] People saw a Kurd [Jalal Talabani] become the president of Iraq and began demanding their cultural and political rights in Syria.'[23]

In the late 1950s, while he was still a member of the KDP, Jalal Talabani often lived in Damascus as the representative of Mulla Mustafa Barzani. The 'conservative' Barzani and 'progressive' Talabani, however, were already rivals to the extent that for many years each had his own partisans within the Kurdish Democratic Party in Syria (KDPS). Talabani, for example, temporarily convinced the KDPS to change its name from Kurdish to Kurdistan, significantly implying that the Kurds in Syria were also part of a transnational entity called Kurdistan, instead of just being some group living in Syria. This, however, was dangerous terminology as it might have led Damascus to believe that the KDPS's ultimate goal was secession. Thus, the KDPS soon reverted to the earlier, more modest term Kurdish. Nevertheless, and despite declining to seek independence, in its early days the KDPS had as part of its programme such transnational goals as the fight against imperialism, support for the Kurdish fights in Turkey, Iraq and Iran, and backing for all oppressed peoples.[24] In addition, there was also the question of whether the KDPS should support Barzani or Talabani, a problem that contributed to the KDPS split in the 1960s.

In the 1970s, Barzani had invited the two KDPS factions to Iraqi Kurdistan in an attempt to reunify them, but this effort ultimately failed. As described above, the Kurdish parties in Syria continued to split into what became a confused host of mostly obscure entities. Nevertheless, those parties with links to the PKK in Turkey or the KDP and PUK in Iraq today contain the largest number of militants, level of finances and thus, in part, legitimacy. To this day portraits of Mulla Mustafa Barzani can be found in people's homes, while his son Massoud—his father's unchallenged successor since the sudden death of his half-brother Idris Barzani of a heart attack in 1987, and president of the KRG since 2005— also commands great respect among Syrian Kurds. Abdullah Ocalan's portrait too can often be seen among the many supporters of the PYD. At the time of writing in 2013, then, the Kurdish Democratic Party of Syria (KDPS) headed by Abdul Hakim Bashar is the sister party of Barzani's KDP. The Kurdish Democratic Progressive Party of Abdul Hamid Darwish plays a similar role with Talabani's PUK, while the PYD of Salih Muslim, as previously mentioned, is affiliated with Abdullah Ocalan's PKK. The KDPS, known as *el-Parti* (the Party) in reference to its claimed descent from the original KDPS—an assertion that several other Kurdish parties could also make—maintains that it is the strongest, but developments since July 2012 would demonstrate that this accolade is now held by the PYD. However, both the KDP and the PUK continue to maintain offices in Syria.

After Mulla Mustafa Barzani died in exile in the United States on 1 March 1979, his two sons Idris and Massoud eventually reconstituted the KDP while, as mentioned above, Jalal Talabani proclaimed his new PUK in Damascus on 1 June 1975. The Barzani-Talabani rivalry was renewed. Idris Barzani arrived in Damascus in 1979 to establish formal relations with Syria. The PUK opened a radio station (The Voice of Revolutionary Kurdistan) in Syria in November 1980 and began broadcasting to Iraq. Damascus offered these opportunities and sanctuary to both KDP and PUK for at least two main reasons: 1.) the intra-Baathist rivalry between Hafez al-Assad's Syria and Saddam Hussein's Iraq; and 2.) the quid pro quo between Syria and the Iraqi Kurds that in return for sanctuary, they would not try to foment rebellion among the Kurds in Syria. It was the same game that Assad later played with the PKK.[25]

Thus, as mentioned above, both the KDP and PUK have continued to maintain offices in Damascus and Qamishli up to the present day. This has allowed the two Iraqi Kurdish parties to hold a gateway in the furthest end of Jazira for journalists and political representatives to pass back and forth between Kurdish areas in Syria and Iraq. Furthermore, since 2003 the KRG has welcomed Kurdish activists exiled from Syria and given them facilities from which they were able to reorganise. Kurdish students expelled from Syrian universities have been admitted to universities in Irbil and Sulaymaniya.

When Jalal Talabani became president of Iraq on 6 April 2005, Kurds living in Damascus played the pan-Kurdish national anthem *Ey Reqib* in celebration.[26] This is a famous Kurdish march that has been adopted by both the KRG and PKK as their official national anthems. It also was the national anthem of the Mahabad Republic of Kurdistan in Iran in 1946. The words to this national hymn were written by the Kurdish Iranian poet Yunis Rauf (also known as Dildar), while the music itself is traditional. The original words were written in the Kurdish dialect of Sorani but were later translated by the famous Kurdish musician Sivan Perwer into Kurmanji. (Sivan Perwer later composed a song about the Syrian Kurdish uprising in Qamishli in 2004, an important event in the Syrian Kurdish narrative that will be discussed in a subsequent chapter.) Thus, *Ey Reqib's* popularity among the Kurds in Syria illustrates how they feel part of the transnational Kurdish nation.

Additional examples of important nationalist events for the Kurds in Syria, some of which are transnational, include: 1.) 1 June, the anniversary of the death of Sheikh Khaznawi (see below); 2.) 5 October, the anniversary of the special census of 1962 that stripped many Kurds of their Syrian citizenship; 3.) 13 November, the anniversary of the Amuda theatre fire in 1960 that killed more than 280 children; 4.) 16 March, the date of the Iraqi poison gas attack on Halabja; 5.) 14 June, the day that the original KDPS was established; and such international holidays as the Day of Human Rights, Labour Day, International Women's Day and Children's Day.

Shortly after Talabani became president of Iraq, the now empowered Massoud Barzani, as newly chosen president of the KRG, called upon Syria to grant the Kurds in Syria their democratic rights. Barzani's actions were a definite break from his past subservience to Syria on this matter. Given their past and continuing transnational importance as models for the demands of the Kurds in Syria, the following two chapters will further analyse the KRG and PKK, and then be followed by another chapter that will examine the all-important role of the United States.

5

THE KRG MODEL

As made clear in the previous chapter about how the Kurds in Syria have been influenced by transnational factors, the KRG in Iraq presents the most successful model of an actual functioning Kurdish state in modern times. Compared with the model of the PKK in Turkey—which will be analysed in the next chapter—the KRG is also a more moderate model as it has successfully pursued first economic and more recently political relations with Turkey, the all-important regional state in the Kurdish past, present and future. Without Turkish co-operation, a Kurdish state is probably impossible. On the other hand, of course, without satisfying Kurdish demands a secure, economically prosperous and democratic Turkey is also unlikely. Clearly the two are involved in a joint win/win future if they can learn to co-operate. The PKK has arrived more slowly at such a possible accommodation, although it opened formal peace talks with the Turkish government early in 2013. The purpose of this chapter is first to analyse recent economic aspects of the KRG model and then segue into a current political analysis. How has the KRG model of the Iraqi Kurds[1] influenced the Kurds in Syria, and to what extent can the Syrian Kurds profit from it?

Recent economic developments

Given the withdrawal of US troops from Iraq at the end of 2011 but increasing resumption of sectarian strife in 2013, what are the KRG's immediate and long-term economic opportunities and prospects?[2] 95 per cent of the Iraqi budget—17 per cent of which goes to the KRG—literally flows from oil, thus making Iraq and the KRG classical rentier states. Thus, the main economic question for the KRG involves the still unanswered problem of the disposition of Iraq's oil resources. Dr Ashti A. Hawrami, the KRG minister for natural resources and a well-known former international oil executive, addressed this issue in a wide-ranging interview in the KRG capital of Irbil (Arbil, Erbil or, in Kurdish, Hawler) on 14 June 2006.[3] His arguments remain pertinent today. Hawrami strongly maintained that Article 115 of the new Iraqi Constitution 'states the supremacy of regional laws over federal laws, and can be invoked if no agreement is reached on the management of oil and gas resources and the distribution of proceeds'. He also argued that Article 112 of the Constitution only permits the Iraqi government 'an administrative role confined to the handling, i.e. exporting and marketing, of the extracted oil and gas from existing producing fields. […] The elected authorities of the regions and producing governorates are now entitled to administer and supervise the extraction process; in other words local oilfield managers are answerable to the local authorities.' Hawrami went on to argue that since the new constitution was silent on undeveloped fields or any new fields, 'the regions and governorates will have all the controls'. Although he stated that the KRG and the government in Baghdad would be able to co-operate, heated verbal conflict over the issue of natural resources continues.

Since Hawrami's speech, several apparent compromises on a hydrocarbons law have fallen through. In June 2009, for example, the KRG actually signed several contracts with foreign companies to extract oil from the Taq Taq and Tawke fields in the KRG region, including one with Norway's DNO as well as Canada's Addax Petroleum (acquired by China Petrochemical) and Turkey's Genel Enerji International.[4] At the time, this development was hailed as an important breakthrough for KRG-Iraq relations as the Kurds said they could produce 200,000 barrels per day (bpd) by the end of 2010, about 10 per cent of Iraq's current output and up from a maximum of 100,000 bpd the previous year. However, the deal fell through over who should pay the foreign oil firms that were developing fields in the KRG region. Nouri al-Maliki's government in Baghdad labelled the deals illicit and declared that the KRG would pay the firms from its percentage of the annual national budget. The KRG declined to go along with this interpretation. In October 2009, the Kurds suspended exports, and the KRG's output subsequently slumped to 20,000 bpd.

In February 2010, however, the KRG and Baghdad finally agreed to resume production and exports, but without an agreement on production-sharing contracts. Crude production from oilfields in Iraqi Kurdistan was announced at 80,000 bpd with 50,000 bpd being exported; the rest was being used for domestic purposes. Production was expected to ramp up quickly to 100,000 bpd.[5] However, the fate of the earlier disputed deals between the KRG and foreign companies remained unclear. Hussain al-Shahristani, the former Iraqi oil minister and the Kurds' nemesis in this situation, claimed that the resumption of oil exports had no connection with finding a solution to the problem of the earlier KRG contracts.[6] In other words, the larger impasse remained.

The second al-Maliki government finally cobbled together in December 2010 appointed al-Shahristani deputy prime minister with overall responsibilities in the energy sector. His increased prominence might bode ill for the Kurds. On the other hand, Abdul-Karim Luaibi, the new Iraqi oil minister, has had less antagonistic relations with Irbil in the past, while acting as the main intermediary in talks between the KRG and Baghdad.

Oil prospects

The second al-Maliki government has ambitiously sought to boost its oil output capacity from 2.5 million bpd to 12 million bpd in the next six or seven years.[7] If successful, this would bring Iraq's production up to that of Saudi Arabia, the global leader. Iraq's current output was only 1.9 bpd million as of November 2010, while the KRG was producing only 100,000 bpd in 2009 when the flow was halted over acrimonious debate with Baghdad concerning the legality of the KRG contracts with foreign oil companies and the mechanism to pay production costs. Early in December 2010, the Kurdish MPs in the Iraqi parliament staged a brief walkout when they learned Baghdad planned to reduce the KRG's share of federal revenues if the KRG failed to produce oil for export in 2011.[8]

Apropos of this situation, however, Ali Hussein, a senior adviser for the KRG's Minister of Natural Resources Ashti Hawrami, announced early in the new year 2011 that the KRG region had an estimated 45 billion barrels of oil reserves.[9] If true, this meant that if the KRG region were independent it would possess the world's sixth largest oil reserves.

Hawrami himself commented about the overall economic situation for the KRG from his point of view:[10] (1) Eight new oil discoveries have been made in the KRG region over the past two to three years. (2) The KRG has signed thirty-seven contracts with forty companies leading to $10 billion of investment in the oil sector regarding exploration and production. Among the most notable were the US companies Marathon Oil and Murphy Oil, the Spanish company Repsol and the Chinese company Sinopec. (3) Three refineries have been commissioned with a total capacity of 200,000 bpd. (4) Three power plants have been built providing 80 per cent of the KRG's energy needs. (5) Kurdish production can reach 1 million bpd by 2014. (6) The KRG also has a potential of some 100–200 trillion standard cubic feet of natural gas. (7) The KRG is ready to start exporting 100,000 bpd and to increase to 150,000 bpd by 2012. (8) At the same time, however, Baghdad's oil production target of 12 million bpd in the next decade will ruin the international oil market by placing too much oil on it. (9) The KRG crude will be exported from two Kurdish fields, from Taq Taq by truck and from Tawke through the existing pipeline to Turkey's Mediterranean seaport of Ceyhan. Indeed, oil was already shipped from these two fields for four months in 2009 until suspended when Baghdad refused to pay back contracting foreign companies.

Further data indicate that the RWE Group AG, Germany's second largest utility, has signed a co-operation agreement with the KRG to help develop the Kurdish region's gas distribution network.[11] Barham Salih, the then KRG prime minister, declared, 'this is a major step forward in our planning. RWE will bring the know-how and insights of one of Europe's most important gas-distribution companies to Kurdistan.' In addition, the German-based company Essen will also provide assistance with the Kurdish region's gas network as well as training local citizens. In the future, the proposed Nabucco Line to Europe that would bypass Russia was to be used, but subsequently was cancelled because of a combination of geopolitical and business factors that lie beyond the scope of this analysis.

Foreign investments

Given the KRG region's progressive investment law, free-market practices and excellent security situation relative to the rest of Iraq, there has been an explosion of foreign investment in the region. In March 2011,

FDI Magazine, a subsidiary of the British *Financial Times*, ranked Irbil fifth among the top Middle East cities in terms of their potential for foreign direct investment (FDI).[12] The rating was based on the cities' economic potential, infrastructure, business friendliness and FDI promotion strategy. The Kurdistan Board of Investment estimated that $17 billion had already been invested in projects ranging from cement factories to shopping malls in the past five years.

Some measure of this burgeoning situation is given by the many companies that participated in a four-day international fair in Irbil at the end of November 2010.[13] Chief among these foreign participants were seventy-six Turkish companies, followed by fifty-three Iranian, forty-four Jordanian, forty-one German, forty-one French, nineteen United Arab Emirates, sixteen Austrian, thirteen Czech, eleven UK, five Chinese, but only two US. In addition, representatives from all seventeen diplomatic contingents present in Irbil attended along with a broadly-based array of senior regional and international personalities. It was the sixth consecutive year that the KRG had hosted the fair whose organisers praised the Kurdish region's relative nearness to Europe and newly opened airline connections[14] as well its business-friendly laws and capable workforce. They also claimed that investment opportunities abounded not only in oil, but also in agriculture, tourism and manufacturing.

The ironic paucity of US investments was largely explained by the relative proximity of Europe and the US State Department's now anachronistic hesitance to even mention the word Kurdistan out of deference to Turkey's Kurdish sensitivities. However, given that on 29 March 2011 Recep Tayyip Erdogan became the first Turkish prime minister to visit the KRG, where he energetically promoted increased business initiatives between the two sides,[15] that approximately 55 per cent of the foreign firms in the Kurdish region—640 out of 1,170—are Turkish, and that the bilateral trade between Turkey and the Kurdish region is projected to grow from $6 billion in 2010 to $20 billion by 2014, the US deference would seem misplaced. This is especially so since Iran is Turkey's main economic and political rival throughout Iraq including the Kurdish region.[16]

Another recent assessment noted that, 'Turkey's influence is greater in northern Iraq and broader, though not deeper, than Iran's in the rest of the country.'[17] Some 15,000 Turks are working in Irbil and other parts of the Kurdish region and Turkish companies make up two-thirds of all foreign firms in the region. Key to Turkey's success has been its projection of its soft power: culture, education and business. 'On the road from Erbil to Baghdad, its pop culture is everywhere.' Ibrahim Tatlises, the famous ethnic Kurdish singer born in Turkey, has lent his portrait to advertisements promoting Turkish-constructed villas. At the Ibrahim Khalil border post between Turkey and the Kurdish region, 1,500 trucks pass daily, carrying Turkish building materials, clothes, furniture and food, to fill the markets of the Kurdish region. As mentioned above, on 29 March 2011, the Turkish Prime Minister Erdogan helped to solidify these fledgling economic and political relations by making an historic visit to Irbil.[18] He was the first Turkish leader to do so.

Full-service banking has been one of the Kurdish region's main problems. Money transfers, for example, are still carried on via primitive methods and many walk around with their pockets stuffed with currency. Vakifbank, a Turkish state-run bank, has now opened a branch in Irbil. Suleyman Kalkan, the director general of Vakifbank, declared, 'There is a great individual banking potential in the region [...] especially in housing and automobile loans.'[19] He added that his bank would also provide commercial and corporate products to meet the finance needs of the Turkish companies operating in the region. Nevertheless, the dearth of full banking services continued into 2013.

Majidi Mall, Iraq's most luxurious shopping mall, opened in Irbil in November 2009.[20] Its outlets include Mango, Ecco, Chopard, Diesel and Levi's, among others. Kuwait City Centre has also opened an anchor store, which immediately became Irbil's most popular hypermarket. A dozen more shopping malls with many international brands have also appeared, largely replacing the famous Qaysaria Bazaar near Irbil's ancient citadel that dates from the twelfth century. International investments have exceeded more than $16 billion. BTWShiells, with more than thirty years of retail experience in London, Dubai and Belfast, is one of the developers of Mane Mall. This shopping complex will offer over 150 brands, a hypermarket, multiplex cinema, bowling lanes and fine-dining experience. Directly linked to it is a 250-room hotel.

Family Fun Mall will also soon open as part of an already popular theme park. It will have space for about 350 renowned brands. The new mall will also host Carrefour, the world's second largest hypermarket chain in terms of size and revenue. The entire complex will be managed by GLL, which operates seventy-five shopping centres around the world, including the largest in Turkey. The quarter of a million expatriates working in the Kurdish region already have such choice living sections as the American Village and the Italian Village in which to reside. Given all these positive factors and its natural geographical attractions, the *New York Times* recently ranked Iraqi Kurdistan as one of the top thirty-four places to visit in the world,[21] while the National Geographic website listed is as number twenty.[22]

Positive too is how Iraq was able to weather more than nine months of governmental impasse following the inconclusive elections of 7 March 2010 without any major security degradation. Iyad Allawi's eventual decision to accept the new al-Maliki government that was finally cobbled together in December 2010 may also be seen in a positive light because his electoral bloc had actually won two more seats in parliament than al-Maliki's. Thus, Allawi's backing for the new government gives it further legitimacy.

Investment contretemps

As noted above, the new al-Maliki government and the KRG continue to struggle with a lack of transparency, conflicts of interest and sheer corruption. Crony capitalism and nepotism are rampant and the public payroll gobbles up approximately three-quarters of the KRG budget. Banking services remain primitive and there is no effective taxation, insurance or postal system. Phone services are very expensive. Baghdad's and Irbil's ambitious plans to expand their oil production face many problems. The current infrastructure is barely adequate to move the modest amount of crude oil currently being produced. Pipelines are old and their capacity is too low. Storage terminals are needed. Ports must be upgraded after years of neglect. Iraq's infrastructure, degraded by decades of war, international sanctions, underinvestment and dictatorial rule, crippled by a badly run centrally-planned economy suffering from endemic shortages of electricity and a population both weary of all these problems and demanding solutions, remains.

What is more, an escalating security challenge continues in the Arab section of Iraq. Al-Maliki's government increasingly looks too narrowly based and cumbersome to be effective. Samuel Ciszuk, the Middle East analyst with IHS Global Insight, has warned that, 'foreign investors will struggle to find enough skilled workers, equipment and material while controlling project costs [...] [and] enough financial resources to resolve the infrastructure bottlenecks for which it is responsible.'[23] In addition, legal uncertainty remains regarding the oil contracts signed by the KRG. What is more, will all the investment projects detailed above in the Kurdish region continue to prosper, or will they prove an illusory bubble and collapse from over-ambitious expansion?

On 17 February 2011, a potentially ominous new factor emerged when the popular uprisings that had already toppled unpopular governments in Tunisia and Egypt reached the KRG.[24] Previously such demonstrations were virtually unheard of in Iraqi Kurdistan. The protestors were demanding better living conditions and anti-corruption efforts. They were attacked by KRG armed forces; at least three people were killed and another 121 wounded. The government defended its violent reaction as self-defence. Hundreds of students in Sulaymaniya University demonstrated, seeking the release of those previously arrested and the prosecution of a local party official who they claimed had ordered security forces to open fire.

Subsequently, masked gunmen attacked and burned Naliya Radio and Television (NRT), an independent TV station located in a gated community called German Village. NRT had aired footage of shots fired at demonstrators during an earlier protest. Twana Osman, the director-general of NRT, declared that the KRG and PUK were clearly to blame for the attack.[25] In addition, Radio Gorran was prevented from broadcasting and the Irbil headquarters of the KNN TV and radio station were set ablaze. Criticisms were specifically levelled against the KRG President Massoud Barzani who responded that the protests were the work of a 'very small group of people determined to undermine the stability of the region'.[26] Subsequently, however, Barzani called for a 'raft of reforms',[27] for creation of an integrity commission to check on corruption and nepotism, and urged early provincial elections for the 111-seat KRG parliament in Irbil. All such reforms have been slow to be implemented, but no further civic unrest on such a scale has occurred in 2013.

Recent political developments

The KRG currently has many of the trappings of an independent state: its own president, prime minister and parliament; its own flag and national anthem; its own army that even prevents Baghdad's army from entering the Kurdish region; its own international airports and an educational system in which few even bother to learn Arabic any more; and even its own stamp entered into the passports of visitors. For the Kurds in Syria, therefore, the KRG may at times appear to be the impossible dream. Still, it is seen by many as a successful model to be either emulated or maybe even joined.

However, many wondered what would happen to the KRG once the remaining US troops were withdrawn from Iraq at the end of 2011. Earlier the KRG and Baghdad had already come perilously close to blows over Kirkuk and their disputed internal border, often referred to as 'the trigger line', the events at Khanaqin in 2008 being a prime example.[28] Despite the US withdrawal, however, the KRG has continued to prosper by gaining increased significance as a type of strategic depth for Turkey against Baghdad and Tehran, and a safe haven for American operations in the region.[29]

In the meantime, moreover, the Iraqi Kurds have had their own Kurdish Spring, first when the anti-corruption *Gorran* (Change) Party split the long-entrenched PUK in the KRG elections held on 25 July 2009, and subsequently when, as detailed above, violent demonstrations broke out in Sulaymaniya, the KRG's second largest city, on 17 February 2011, and continued until forcibly curtailed by the KRG leadership on 19 April 2011.

Most of the demonstrators were protesting against corruption, nepotism and the lack of effective services such as jobs and electricity. Intellectuals and journalists also protested against limitations of free speech and press freedom, as well as daily harassment. Among all there was a deep anger against the KDP and PUK family domination over society and government.[30]

Unlike the targets of the Arab Spring demonstrators, however, the KRG had just been democratically elected in July 2009 and thus was not so readily able to be denounced as illegitimate. The KRG also was able to prevent demonstrations from breaking out in Irbil, its capital and largest city, by closing the universities, sending the students home and banning large gatherings. Nevertheless, the anti-KRG demonstrations that did occur constituted a serious wake-up call that all was not well with the KRG. As Barham Salih, the KRG prime minister from 2009 to 2012, declared, 'We must do better. Our citizens demand better, and they deserve better.'[31]

Barzani hints at independence

In return for vague promises to support the KRG's agenda regarding the disputed city and province of Kirkuk as well as oil revenue, the Kurds played a major role in helping Nouri al-Maliki form his new, second government at the end of 2010. At a KDP conference in Irbil to help patch Maliki's new coalition together, at which Maliki was in attendance, the KRG President Massoud Barzani declared that the Iraqi Kurdish region had the right of self-determination.[32] Such a right usually implies independence although it could also lead to the type of self-chosen autonomy the Kurds already exercised.

As soon as Maliki assumed power again, and against the backdrop of the final US troop withdrawal at the end of 2011, relations between Baghdad and the KRG began to deteriorate. Solutions to the perennial issues of Kirkuk and the sharing of oil revenue[33] proved elusive. In addition, since Maliki was unable to complete his new cabinet, he personally also assumed control of several leading ministries, leading to charges of nascent dictatorship. Then, in January 2012, Maliki issued a warrant for the arrest of Vice President Tariq al-Hashemi, the highest ranking Sunni in his Shiite-dominated government, on charges of having led death squads. Hashemi denied the charges and fled to the Kurdish region where he was granted protection. US Senator John McCain, who had been the unsuccessful Republican candidate against President Barack Obama in 2008, noted the rising tensions and declared that, 'the situation in Iraq is unraveling. […] Iraq will likely break up which would eventually lead to the formation of three different States.'[34] Although Obama's vice president Joseph Biden would not have liked to be reminded of it, McCain's three-state solution was similar to what he had earlier adumbrated, but now opposed.[35]

In a flurry of activity, Barzani journeyed to the United States, Turkey and Europe for well-publicised meetings. His talks in Turkey were especially noteworthy given how relations between the two sides had improved so dramatically in the past few years. Turkey was now taking the KRG's side in disputes with Baghdad. The Turkish Prime Minister Recep Tayyip Erdogan accused Maliki of fanning tensions in Iraq with the Kurds, while Maliki denounced Turkey for its 'flagrant interference in Iraqi internal affairs'.[36] The following month, Nechirvan Barzani, the new KRG prime minister and the nephew of Massoud Barzani, also journeyed to Turkey for yet another high-level Turkish-KRG meeting. With such Turkish support, some speculated that the KRG might indeed be emboldened to secede from a crumbling Iraq.[37]

Back in Irbil, Barzani suggested that Baghdad might use the 18 F-16 fighter jets it was scheduled to purchase from the United States to once again subjugate the Kurds.[38] The KRG president demanded that Maliki agree on sharing power with his political opponents by September 2012 'or else the Kurds could consider breaking away from Baghdad'. There was a 'very dangerous political crisis in the country', and unless the impasse was broken 'voters in the Kurdish region may consider a referendum for a state independent of Iraq'.[39] Barzani also supported an Iraqi parliamentary motion to remove Maliki from office. However, Jalal Talabani, Barzani's old Kurdish nemesis and now president of Iraq, successfully opposed the motion to remove Maliki.

In November 2012, a sudden new crisis erupted as tensions mounted over the formation of Baghdad's Dijla Operations Command, a new military formation that was to operate in the area over which both Baghdad and the KRG claimed jurisdiction. Troops from the two sides faced off in what one report declared was 'a crisis that [...] could erupt into a full-blown war',[40] before tensions were defused. How often, however, could Baghdad and the KRG keep dodging the bullet?

Despite Barzani's bellicosity, most observers felt that he was really manoeuvring for position in post-US-occupied Iraq. Premature Kurdish independence that would be seen as destroying Iraq would be opposed by not only the United States, but all the KRG's regional neighbours. What is more, the KRG continued to enjoy in federal Iraq all the advantages of independence without its disadvantages. It would be far better for the Iraqi Kurds to be seen as doing their utmost to keep Iraq united. Only if the Kurds' best efforts failed and Iraq still split apart would the Kurds then be seen as having had independence forced upon them and therefore being justified. Patience and astute diplomacy remained the main call words.

On 18 December 2012 Jalal Talabani, president of Iraq, suffered a debilitating stroke. Mam Jalal, as he affectionately was called, had worked successfully to help keep Iraq united and had also just met Nouri al-Maliki in an attempt to ease tensions between the KRG and Baghdad over the territories disputed between them and the disposition of the oil reserves. What would the removal of Talabani's calming and astute abilities mean?

In the event, KRG relations with Baghdad have stabilised. In 2013, both President Massoud Barzani and Prime Minister Nechirvan Barzani met Maliki in Baghdad. Although no solutions to the basic underlying problems have been reached, they were able to defuse tensions, at least for the time being.

Regarding the continuing civil war in Syria and what it meant for the Kurds who lived there, Massoud Barzani continued to play an active role. Seeking to mediate while also being buttressed by the support of his *de facto* allies Turkey and the United States, Barzani also sought to call a pan-Kurdish conference in Irbil that would include all of the Kurds in Syria as well as the PKK. This gathering would certainly seek to provide guidance and leverage for the Syrian Kurds. Although past experiences indicated that no conclusive answers would be forthcoming, the KRG model for the Kurdish future in Syria would certainly be prominently displayed.

At the time of writing, in December 2013, the pan-Kurdish conference has been thrice postponed amid intra-Kurdish differences over how to allocate representation to the different groups, among other points, and is unlikely to be held in the near future. Barzani's KRG model and Ocalan's PKK model have become the two great rivals for leadership of the pan-Kurdish movement, a struggle reflected in the Syrian civil war, and the failure to convene the pan-Kurdish conference in Irbil or to agree upon Kurdish representation at a proposed Geneva II meeting on the Syrian civil war, now scheduled in January 2014. Indeed, on 16–17 November 2013, Barzani even met with the Turkish prime minister Erdogan in Diyarbakir, Turkey in an apparent effort to reduce the PKK role in the ongoing Turkish–Kurdish (PKK) peace process that had begun earlier that year. By using the ancient technique of divide and rule, Erdogan appeared to be seeking to split and weaken the Kurdish movement in Turkey and Syria, and thus make it more applicable to his wishes not only in regards to the current peace process in Turkey but also in the many other avenues of Middle Eastern politics dealing with KRG energy resources and the continuing civil war in Syria. However, to the extent that Erdogan was trying to use Barzani to marginalise the PKK, the Turkish strategy would fail because the PKK was the main Kurdish party in Turkey, not Barzani's Iraqi KDP.

Leyla Zana and Osman Baydemir, two moderate Turkish-Kurdish leaders with ties to the PKK, journeyed to Irbil in December 2013. There they met with Barzani in an effort to bring the KRG and PKK together in regards to policy affecting the Syrian Kurds. Salih Muslim, the co-chair of the PYD, welcomed this initiative, but emphasised that the Syrian Kurds possessed the ultimate power to decide on matters relating to their future. The PYD/PKK was in a strong position given its recent victories over Islamic jihadists and Salafists groups in recent months. At this point, however, the present analysis will turn to the PKK model as it applies to the Kurds in Syria.

6

THE PKK MODEL

Compared to the KRG model, that of the PKK or Kurdistan Workers Party is more radical and less successful as it has not resulted in achieving an actual state or even obtaining full democratic rights yet for its constituency. Nevertheless, the PKK struggle that began in August 1984 has in some very important ways galvanised all aspects of Kurdish society even more than the KRG has, the active participation of women in the PKK being a prime example. Furthermore, now that the PKK has entered into peace negotiations with Turkey, its model would seem even more viable. This may prove to be all the more true if these peace negotiations prove successful because then the PKK affiliate in Syria—PYD—will be in a position to benefit in its heretofore troubled relations with Turkey. Already, for example, on 25 July 2013 Salih Muslim, the PYD leader, was invited to Istanbul to discuss his vision for the Kurdish future in Syria. Such a visit would have been inconceivable just a few months earlier. Much more, of course, has to happen, but clearly, given the incredible success of the PYD to date, the PKK model also holds relevance for the Kurds in Syria. To appreciate the situation in more depth, this chapter will examine the PKK.

Brief historical background

The effort to find a solution to the Kurdish problem in Turkey is nothing new. It has been continuing ever since the PKK—formally founded on 27 November 1978—began its violent uprising on 15 August 1984.[1]

Over the years the PKK goals have evolved from initial plans to establish an independent Marxist state to current ones for the recognition of Kurdish political, social and cultural rights within a decentralised Turkey. However, Turkey has long considered the PKK a terrorist movement, a designation also accepted by its allies, the United States and the EU. Therefore, in most cases the efforts to achieve peace simply amounted to attempts to impose it by military means and thus, until recently, without any meaningful political reforms.

Nevertheless, over the years, the PKK had declared numerous unilateral ceasefires with the stated intention of having them lead to peace negotiations. In most cases, Turkey ignored these PKK ceasefires, deeming them mere signs of PKK weakness and imminent defeat.[2] The only important exception occurred in March 1993, when the then Turkish President Turgut Ozal appeared close to accepting one of these PKK ceasefire offers to negotiate. Ozal's sudden death on 17 April 1993, however, ended this effort and even heavier fighting soon ensued.

Turkey's increasing military pressure in the late 1990s finally led to the PKK leader Ocalan being forced out of his safe house in Syria in October 1998 and his eventual capture by Turkish commandos in Nairobi, Kenya on 15 February 1999.[3] At this time, Ocalan's capture seemed to end the conflict. The PKK declared another ceasefire and withdrew its forces from Turkey into the largely inaccessible Qandil mountains of northern Iraq bordering on Iran. However, Turkey continued to dismiss PKK offers to negotiate and demanded what amounted to a total surrender. By the summer of 2004, violence had begun again and it gradually escalated, so that by 2012 there were more deaths from the fighting than at any time since the late 1990s.

However, in the summer of 2009, the Kurdish problem in Turkey[4] seemed on the verge of a solution when the ruling Adalet ve Kalkinma Partisi (Justice and Development Party) or AKP[5] government of Prime Minister Recep Tayyip Erdogan and President Abdullah Gul announced a Kurdish Opening or Initiative (also known as as the Democratic Opening/Initiative). Gul declared that 'the biggest problem of Turkey is the Kurdish question' and that 'there is an opportunity [to solve it] and it should not be missed'.[6] Erdogan asked, 'If Turkey had not spent its energy, budget, peace and young people on [combating] terrorism, if Turkey had not spent the last 25 years in conflict, where would we be today?'[7] Even the insurgent PKK, still led ultimately by its imprisoned leader Abdullah

Ocalan, itself briefly took Turkey's Kurdish Opening seriously.[8] For a fleeting moment optimism ran rampant. What happened?

Problems

Shortly after its initial announcement, it became evident that the AKP government had not thought its Kurdish Opening out very well and then proved rather inept in trying to implement it. Specific proposals were lacking. Furthermore, despite AKP appeals to support its Kurdish Opening, all three of the parliamentary opposition parties declined. Indeed, the Cumhuriyet Halk Partisi (CHP) or Republican Peoples Party (Kemalists or Nationalists) accused the AKP of 'separatism, cowing to the goals of the terrorist PKK, violating the Constitution, causing fratricide and/or ethnic polarisation between Kurds and Turks, being an agent of foreign states, and even betraying the country',[9] while the Milliyetci Haraket Partisi (MHP) or Nationalist Action Party (Ultra Turkish Nationalists) 'declared AKP to be dangerous and accused it of treason and weakness'.[10] Even the pro-Kurdish Demokratik Toplum Partisi (DTP) or Democratic Society Party failed to be engaged because it declined to condemn the PKK as the AKP government had demanded.[11] Erdogan too began to fear that any perceived concessions to the Kurds would hurt his Turkish nationalist base and future presidential hopes.

The PKK's 'peace group' gambit on 18 October 2009 to return thirty-four PKK members home to Turkey from northern Iraq also backfired badly when these Kurdish expatriates were met by huge welcoming receptions at the Habur Border Crossing with Turkey and later in Diyarbakir. These celebrations were broadcast throughout Turkey and proved too provocative for even moderate Turks who perceived the affair as some sort of PKK victory parade. The Peace Group affair seemed to prove that the government had not thought out the implications of its Kurdish Opening and could not manage its implementation, let alone consequences.

Then on 11 December 2009 the Constitutional Court, after mulling over the issue for more than two years, suddenly banned the pro-Kurdish DTP because of its close association with the PKK. Although the Baris ve Demokrasi Partisi (BDP) or Peace and Democracy Party quickly took the DTP's place, the state-ordered banning of the pro-Kurdish DTP could not have come at a worse time, and put the kiss of death on the Kurdish Opening. In addition, more than 1,000 BDP and other Kurdish notables were placed under arrest for their supposed support of the PKK, yet another body blow to the Kurdish Opening.[12] Soon the entire country was ablaze from the fury that had arisen, and the Kurdish Opening seemed closed. The entire Kurdish question seemed to have been set back to square one.[13]

In May 2010, the Kurdistan National Congress (KNK), an arm of the PKK, charged that since April 2009 more than 1,500 politicians, human rights advocates, writers, artisans and leaders of civil society organisations had been arrested. In addition, 4,000 children had been taken to court and 400 of them imprisoned for participating in demonstrations. Osman Baydemir, the popular ethnic Kurdish mayor of Diyarbakir, was scheduled to go to court on charges of 'membership in a terror organisation', while Muharrem Erbey, the vice chairman of Turkey's largest human rights organisation the Human Rights Association, had already been imprisoned. And Jess Hess, an American freelance journalist, had been deported for reporting critically on human rights abuses against the Kurds.[14]

Renewed problems

Although the AKP won practically 50 per cent of the popular vote or 326 seats[15] while the BDP and its allies won a record thirty-six seats[16] in the parliamentary elections held on 12 June 2011, further problems soon arose and hopes for a renewed and more successful Kurdish Opening quickly foundered. Secretive talks between Ocalan in his prison on the island of Imrali[17] and other senior PKK leaders in Oslo with Turkish intelligence officials from the National Intelligence Organisation broke down.[18] Violence flared to heights not reached since the late 1990s.

Ocalan's proposals

Although Ocalan's 160-page roadmap for solving the Kurdish problem was confiscated by the Turkish authorities in August 2009 and therefore never even submitted, its contents are largely known on the basis of his earlier testimony at his trial for treason in 1999[19] and subsequent statements over the years.[20] In essence, the imprisoned PKK leader has proposed a democratisation and decentralisation of the Turkish state into what he has termed at various times a democratic republic, a democratic confederalism, a democratic nation or a democratic homeland. Such autonomy and decentralisation would be based on the guidelines already listed in the European Charter of Local Self-Government adopted in 1985 and presently ratified by forty-one states including Turkey—with numerous important conditions, however—and the European Charter of Regional Self-Government, which is still only in draft form. Thus, one might actually argue that earlier BDP proposals for some local autonomy would be bringing Turkey into conformity with EU guidelines by giving the Kurds local self-government. With regard to the Kurds in Syria, moreover, the PKK-affiliated PYD was on record as proposing a similar type of arrangement.[21] Moreover, one might also argue that the *millet* system of autonomous self-government under religious leaders in the former Ottoman Empire offered a historical model for local autonomy or proto-federalism in Turkey.

However, the AKP was appalled when the pro-Kurdish Democratic Society Congress (DTK)—a new non-governmental organisation which is close to the PKK and BDP—met in Diyarbakir in mid-December 2010 and outlined its solution for democratic autonomy, which envisaged Kurdish as a second official language, a separate flag and a Marxist-style organisational model for Kurdish society. The DTK's draft also broached the vague idea of 'self-defence forces' that would be used not only against external forces but in opposition to the subjects of the so-called democratic autonomy initiative who were not participating in what was called the 'struggle'.[22]

The Turkish Republic created by Kemal Ataturk in 1923 has always been a strongly centralised state. Radical decentralisation as proposed by the PKK and BDP goes against this strong mindset and thus would be most problematic. On the other hand, many states such as Britain and France, famous for their centralised unitary structure, have recently rolled back centuries of constitutional forms in favour of what they saw as necessary decentralisation. Far from leading to their break-up as states, this decentralisation has satisfied local particularisms and checked possible demands for future independence. Thus, far from threatening its national unity, some Turkish decentralisation might help preserve it.

However, more than half of Turkey's ethnic Kurdish population does not even live in its historic south-eastern Anatolian homeland but is scattered throughout the country, especially in such cities as Istanbul. In addition, a sizeable number of Turkey's ethnic Kurds have mostly assimilated into a larger Turkish civic identity. Therefore, radical decentralisation that would be incompatible with modern Turkey's heritage may not be necessary. What is needed, however, is for the state to begin seriously talking with the most important, genuine representatives of its disaffected Kurdish minority. This, of course, means the PKK.

However, if Turkey is going to resume negotiating with Ocalan and the PKK, the time must surely come for Turkey to cease terming the PKK a terrorist organisation and instead challenge it to negotiate peacefully. The terrorism appellation distorts the discussion and not only prevents the two main parties to the problem from fully negotiating with each other, but also impairs the EU and US efforts to play a stronger role in achieving peace.

Shortly after the election results of June 2011 had been announced, the newly elected Prime Minister Erdogan seemingly turned his back on an earlier promise to seek consensus on the drafting of a new constitution that would help solve the Kurdish problem, broke off contact with the BDP, and continued to declare that the Kurdish problem had been solved and only a PKK problem remained. How could the new AKP government begin to solve the Kurdish problem when it refused to deal with its main interlocutor?[23]

Then on 14 July 2011 the DTK, the umbrella pro-Kurdish NGO mentioned above, proclaimed 'democratic autonomy', a declaration that seemed wildly premature and over-blown to many observers and infuriated Turkish officialdom. Amidst mutual accusations concerning who was initiating the renewed violence and warlike rhetoric,[24] the Turkish military launched several days of cross-border attacks on reputed PKK targets in northern Iraq's Qandil mountains on 17 August 2011. The Turkish government claimed to have killed 100 Kurdish rebels, while the PKK maintained that it had lost only three fighters and that in addition seven local Iraqi Kurdish civilians had also been killed.[25]

Violence continued on 19 June 2012 when the PKK attacked Diglica, a Turkish outpost near the Iraqi frontier, and killed eight soldiers while wounding another sixteen.[26] The same outpost had been hit five years earlier, so the latest strike seemed to illustrate the lack of Turkish progress in controlling the violence which many saw as a result of the state's failure to negotiate with the PKK.

Others argued, however, that even more, the ultimate problem was the inherent ethnic Turkish inability to accept the fact that Turkey should be considered a multi-ethnic state in which the Kurds have similar constitutional rights as co-stakeholders with the Turks. Moreover, during 2011 and 2012, more leading intellectuals had been rounded up for alleged affiliations with the KCK/PKK,[27] whose proposals for democratic autonomy seem to suggest an alternative government. Many of those arrested were also affiliated with the BDP.

In addition, Leyla Zana, the famous female Kurdish leader and BDP member of parliament, was once again sentenced to prison on 24 May 2012 for 'spreading propaganda' on behalf of the PKK. The charges concerned nine speeches she had made over the years during which she had argued for recognition of the Kurdish identity, called Ocalan a Kurdish leader and urged the reopening of peace negotiations between Turkey and the PKK. Previously in 1994, Zana had been stripped of her membership in parliament and imprisoned for ten years on similar charges. Such renewed Turkish actions reminded one of what the French used to say about the Bourbons: 'They learned nothing and they forgot nothing.'

However, for the time being Zana remained free given her current parliamentary immunity. Interestingly, Zana shortly afterwards declared that she had confidence in Erdogan's ability to solve the Kurdish problem.[28] On 30 June 2012 she actually met with the Turkish prime minister, an event that caused bitter debate within the Kurdish community, but to this author seemed a positive step.[29]

These arrests and sentences point to serious problems. First, there is the nature of the crimes, which allege no violence. Mere 'association' is enough to be counted as a terrorist. In addition, the connections are tenuous. As Human Rights Watch has noted, 'There is scant evidence to suggest the defendants engaged in any acts that could be defined as terrorism as it is understood in international law'.[30] Second, the arrests come at a time when Turkey is planning to develop a new constitution.[31] The silencing of pro-Kurdish voices as constitutional debates go forward is counter-productive for Turkey's future. Finally, there is the way suspects are treated. Virtually all are subject to pre-trial detention, effectively denying them freedom without any proof that they have committed a crime. Although precise figures are unavailable, Human Rights Watch has declared that several thousand are currently on trial and another 605 in pretrial detention on KCK/PKK-related charges.[32]

Reopening?

Recent events offer cautious hope that the time to renew the dialogue and resume direct negotiations between the Turkish government and the PKK may have arrived. In late October 2012, for example, a report in *Zaman*, a respected news outlet, declared that, 'the government is preparing to launch a new initiative to deal with the Kurdish problem to hopefully pave the way for arms to be buried for good.'[33] The *Zaman* report went on to say that the government had learned from the past what steps would not work. It concluded cryptically that, 'therefore, actors and factors that had a part in the previous peace process will not be included in the new process, while for some other actors the government will reach a decision based on observation of the present attitude of those actors'.

The civil war in Syria might also be encouraging a reopening of Turkey's closed Kurdish Opening. In July 2012, as previously mentioned, the embattled Assad regime in Syria suddenly pulled its troops out of Syria's largely north-eastern Kurdish-populated area. A de facto Syrian Kurdish autonomy quickly settled in. At first, Turkey showed its traditional hostility to this development lest it negatively influence Turkey's own disaffected Kurds to make similar demands for autonomy. However, a more nuanced Turkish position surely required a settlement with its own disaffected Kurds to insulate Turkey from the increasing Syrian instability threatening to overflow from Turkey's southern border. Such a settlement also would make the Kurdish situation within Syria less problematic for Turkey.

In late October 2012, Erdogan's visit to Turkey's south-eastern Kurdish-populated region led to speculation that he was about to start a new Opening to solve the Kurdish problem. Erdogan had already said he was ready to relaunch talks with Abdullah Ocalan, the PKK leader still jailed on the island of Imrali. Indeed, Erdogan even declared that the Turkish intelligence service could 'do anything at any moment. [...] For example, if it is necessary to go to Imrali tomorrow, I will tell the MIT [National Intelligence Organization] chief to go ahead.'[34] Hasip Kaplan, a leading BDP MP, actually suggested that new negotiations were already underway, 'I presume that talks on Imrali have started anew.'

Another reason for Erdogan's new-found interest in reopening Turkey's closed Kurdish Opening might be the upcoming Turkish local elections scheduled for early in 2014. Erdogan's AKP and the pro-Kurdish

BDP were expected to be the main rivals for support in Turkey's south-eastern Kurdish region. During the prime minister's recent visit to this area, he reminded the locals that his governing AKP was in a better position to provide basic services for them than the opposition pro-Kurdish nationalist BDP. The immediate question was whether the national elections of 2007, when the AKP party prevailed over the BDP's DTP predecessor in the region, or the 2009 local elections and 2011 national elections, when the DTP/BDP trumped the AKP in the region, would attract the voters.

Indeed, by January 2013, it was clear that the Turkish government had reopened its closed Kurdish Opening and tentative negotiations with Imrali (Ocalan's prison) had begun.[35] The sudden murder of three PKK activists in Paris on 10 January 2013 appeared to be an attempt to sabotage these negotiations.[36] Nevertheless, subsequent reports indicated that officials from the MIT were already meeting again with such prominent PKK leaders in Europe as Sabri Ok, while other negotiations involved Ocalan.[37]

By the beginning of March 2013, these contacts seemed to be moving forward when a BDP group arrived in Sulaymaniya in Iraqi-Kurdish-ruled northern Iraq to deliver a message from Ocalan to the PKK guerrilla leaders ensconced in the Qandil mountains bordering Iraq and Iran.[38] A similar letter was sent to senior PKK leaders in Europe. In his letter, Ocalan spoke about a ceasefire, withdrawing PKK fighters from Turkey, the release of PKK prisoners, disarming and reintegrating some 7,000 PKK fighters into Turkish society, and constitutional reforms.

In doing so, the imprisoned PKK leader struck both optimistic and pessimistic positions: 'Everybody should know that we will neither live nor fight as we used to. […] You should know well that neither I nor the state will take a step back. [We will achieve] a historic peace and transition to democratic life.' Ocalan then explained that, 'the PKK's withdrawal from Turkey will be after a Parliament ruling and the Turkish Grand Assembly will approve it, a truth commission will be established. [Kurdish people who were exiled from their villages] will return to their villages. If these conditions are not met, the [PKK's] withdrawal will not become real.' Ocalan also elaborated on the subsequent political environment he expected after 'the establishment of peace…. Neither house arrest nor amnesty, there will be no need for those. We will all be free.' However, if the peace process fails, 'a civil war will begin with 50,000 people.'

As for the Turkish side, public opinion polls showed that the reopened Kurdish peace talks had tentative public support, a great change from the past when any such suggestions were liable to bring accusations of treason. Gradually the Turkish government has begun to humanise Ocalan in an effort to pave the way for talks. Ocalan's successful call for some 600 supporters to end a hunger strike that was creating dangerous repercussions for the government in the autumn of 2012 is one good example.

In addition, Erdogan declared that, 'if drinking poison hemlock is necessary, we can also drink it to bring peace and welfare to this country.'[39] AKP member of parliament from Diyarbakir Galip Ensarioglu said that, 'Ocalan is more reasonable than those who are outside. Ocalan is acting responsibility and is a chance for Turkey.'[40] Dr Hakan Fidan,[41] the head of MIT—who was involved in the earlier Oslo talks with senior PKK leaders—has been speaking with Ocalan since late 2012. According to Ayla Akat, a BDP MP who recently visited Ocalan, 'Fidan and Ocalan have managed to understand each other.'[42]

Background preparation has already brought Turks and Kurds together in Britain and Ireland to learn about the successful Good Friday Accords that finally brought peace to Northern Ireland's ancient quarrel.[43] Erdogan has approved these contacts. One such visit was to the Scottish Parliament in Edinburgh to see how power might be devolved from the centre successfully, a point crucial in the current bargaining between Turkey and the PKK. The Turkish government has also established a cross-departmental agency to coordinate policy and responses concerning the Kurdish question from security to education and social policy. The agency's head was a recent participant in the visits to Britain.

For its part, the European Parliament endorsed the reopened Kurdish peace process in a special session in which Lucinda Creighton, an Irish politician speaking for the EU presidency, stated, 'It is clear that the wider Kurdish issue can only be addressed through a peaceful, comprehensive and sustainable solution.'[44] Stefan Fule, the EU enlargement commissioner, added that the reopened talks were 'historic [...] [and] would have a strong impact on the [EU] accession process of Turkey as such, as it would further consolidate the role of the European Union as a benchmark for reforms in Turkey.'

Unfortunately, these hopes for a successful conclusion of Turkey's reopening of its closed Kurdish Opening appear tenuous for several reasons. Enormous differences between the two sides remain. The AKP government seeks to solve the issue by having the PKK disarm and its fighters involved in previous violence seek asylum in other countries in exchange for merely removing legal restrictions on the Kurdish identity and language. The PKK, however, wants meaningful autonomy that would give their supporters including Ocalan himself significant power. If the historical record is any guide, the Turkish government will never be willing to grant such concessions which would seem to be leading to the state's break-up. In addition, disarming the PKK as Turkey seeks will prove exceedingly difficult, especially given the PKK's stated position that it should have a role in maintaining security in Turkey's south-eastern Kurdish provinces. One ironic facet to all this is Erdogan's flirting with Ocalan about gaining his and the BDP's support for a new super-presidential Turkish constitution in which Erdogan would occupy this new position. Ocalan, however, has responded about the need for American-style checks and balances.[45]

All this leads to whether the costs of the current fighting are really so high as to demand a settlement. Probably they are not. As Nihat Ali Ozcan, a Turkish counter-terrorist official, has asserted, 'We can tolerate 500 deaths a year. It's considered normal.'[46] Indeed, there remain many elements in both Turkey's security-minded Deep State and its PKK equivalent that actually see themselves as benefiting from the continuance of the fighting. Surely neither side is ready to surrender its key positions for an unfavourable peace that would be seen as a betrayal to all the suffering that has been endured.

Finally, even if Ocalan agrees to a settlement, it is unclear whether he would be able to bring the hardcore PKK guerrillas in the Qandil mountains, and others, along with him. After all the titular PKK leader has grown old as a prisoner in Imrali for more than fourteen years. New PKK leadership and cadres have come of age and are unlikely to meekly give up their positions on the mere words of a person many probably see as out of touch with current realities. Ocalan can be still accepted as titular PKK leader while imprisoned, but if he would actually seek to become the arbitrator of real, daily events, it might be a very different situation. Indeed, Ocalan himself recently suggested that his colleagues in the Qandil mountains were not as enthusiastic about his peace efforts: 'Even the PKK does not understand me […] Qandil is pessimistic, it would be good if they get over it […] I'm angry with them.'[47] Thus, although the current reopening offers a historic opportunity,[48] clearly there remain many serious obstacles to overcome before any permanent settlement can be reached. Nevertheless, the difficult process towards peace has been continuing at the time of writing (September 2013).

7

THE UNITED STATES

Overview

Although Turkey is often the most important state regarding the Kurds, given its immense power and continuing involvement in Middle Eastern politics, the United States is clearly also very important and of course potentially the most so. While Turkey's involvement has been analysed above and will be further below, this situation regarding the United States now warrants a closer analysis.

The United States does not really have any grand foreign policy strategy towards the Kurds because they live in four separate states (Turkey, Iraq, Iran and Syria), each one of which requires its own separate considerations. What is more, the states in which the Kurds live are usually more important for US foreign policy. The Kurds cause problems for the United States when it deals with these more important states. Nevertheless, given its interest in Middle East stability as well as human rights, the United States has come to accept that it does owe the Kurds a certain amount of attention and even protection. This has been true especially in Iraq given the way the Iraqi Kurds supported the United States in the 2003 war against Saddam Hussein when others such as Turkey did not. Indeed the virtually independent KRG in Iraq largely owes its very existence to the United States.

Despite its support for the Iraqi Kurds, however, the United States opposes independence for the Iraqi Kurds, because it feels that this would lead to the partition and end of Iraq and thus to greater instability in the

Middle East. The United States position on this point is all the more adamant given the attitudes of other states such as Turkey and the various Arab governments, all of which oppose Kurdish independence as a threat to their own territorial integrity. The United States tentatively does support the KRG as a way to maintain the political unity of Iraq and satisfy the Kurds. This position, of course, can be inherently contradictory and is a very fine line to tread successfully, especially given the new de facto Turkish-KRG alliance.

Many observers emphasise how much the Iraqi Kurds love the Americans. This needs to be qualified because the Kurds remember that earlier they were twice betrayed by the United States, in 1975 and again in 1991, and therefore they might be again. Indeed, some Kurds began to fear the worst when the Baker-Hamilton Iraq Study Group Report (December 2006) suggested that the hard-won Kurdish federal state might have to be sacrificed to the perceived need for a re-established centralised Iraqi state.[1] Fortunately, for the Kurds, the Report's recommendations were not adopted by the United States, but their mere consideration illustrated how tenuous future US support might be.

On the other hand, US Secretary of Defense Robert Gates acknowledged in a meeting on 11 December 2010 with KRG President Massoud Barzani that Kurdish co-operation is indispensable for the successful implementation of security and strategic framework agreements between the United States and Iraq, and essential for a unified and peaceful Iraq.[2] Even more importantly, the US Obama administration a few days later publicly committed itself to broker disputes between the KRG and the Baghdad government and also help resolve the Kirkuk issue, since the Kurds had agreed to accept the new Iraqi election law that slightly reduced the number of seats the KRG would have in the new Iraqi parliament to be elected in March 2010.[3]

Thus, the United States sees the KRG as a friend and de facto ally, but not as important an ally as it still sees Turkey to be. Therefore, the message is clear. The KRG must get along with Turkey or else, in a showdown between the two, the KRG will not be able to count on US support. Fortunately for the Iraqi Kurds, Turkey's supposed zero-problems with its neighbours' foreign policy means that Turkey is beginning to accept the KRG politically as a friend rather than a security threat as had been the earlier view. Clearly, however, the Kurdish question holds only a minor position in relation to the national security of the United States and the democratisation process it pursues in the Middle East.

Given its relatively weak hand by comparison with Turkey and the Baghdad government, therefore, the KRG lobby in the United States has made a good impression and achieved successes. Qubad Talabani, the KRG representative in the United States until 2012, made a good impression and was able to gain much goodwill for the Kurds. Unfortunately for the KRG, it had not appointed a successor to Qubad Talabani as of December 2013. Nevertheless, KRG relations with the United States remain positive.

On the other hand, rightly or wrongly, the Turkish Kurds are often perceived in the United States as too closely tied to the PKK, which the United States considers to be a terrorist organisation. As a result, the cause of the Turkish Kurds in the United States has not prospered as well as that of their brothers and sisters to the south. This is all the more so given the longstanding US alliance with Turkey. The United States has paid even less attention to the Kurds in Iran, although they might one day serve as a potential ally against the Islamic government in much the same way as the Iraqi Kurds did against Saddam Hussein's Iraq. As for the Kurds in Syria, they were clearly off the radar until Kurdish autonomy occurred in July 2012. Even subsequently, however, the United States has shown little interest in the Kurds of Syria because of its deference to Turkish sensitivities and a vision of a united Syria contributing to stability. On the other hand, the Syrian Kurds are keenly aware of the United States' all-important role and would dearly like to win its support.

With this brief overview and its caveats in mind, the purpose of this chapter is to analyse what might be called the six stages of American foreign policy towards the Kurds.[4] The first three of these stages involving Woodrow Wilson's promises, Mulla Mustafa Barzani's era and the 1991 US war against Iraq have been completed, while the last three concerning the KRG in Iraq since 2003, Turkey and the PKK, and Syria are a continuing process. Although the main concern of this book is the Kurds in Syria, a survey of US policy towards the other Kurds is necessary to understand its all important policy toward the Syrian Kurds.

First stage

American foreign policy involvement with the Kurds dates back to the First World War and President Woodrow Wilson's famous Fourteen Points, the twelfth of which concerned a forlorn promise of 'autonomy' for 'the other nationalities [of the Ottoman Empire] which are now under Turkish rule'.[5] Resurgent Kemalist Turkey's successful struggle to regain its territorial integrity,[6] and Britain's decision to maintain control over the oil-rich Kurdish region of northern Iraq known as the Mosul *vilayet*, however ended nascent Kurdish hopes for independence or even some type of autonomy.[7] The first brief Wilsonian stage or prelude to American foreign policy towards the Kurds had ended.

Second stage

A half century passed before American foreign policy again became involved with the Kurds. Because of the North Atlantic Treaty Alliance (NATO), the United States supported the position of the Turkish government on the Kurdish issue in that state. This was to deny Kurdish demands for minority rights as they might escalate into further demands that would threaten Turkish territorial integrity.[8] Thus, the Kurds who supported the PKK in Turkey became 'bad Kurds' from the point of view of American foreign policy.[9]

In Iraq, however, in what might be called the second or Mulla Mustafa Barzani stage in American foreign policy towards the Kurds, the United States encouraged and, to a certain extent, even supported Barzani's revolt against Iraq during the early 1970s.[10] Thus, the Iraqi Kurds became the 'good Kurds' from the point of view of American foreign policy. The United States pursued this policy for several reasons: (1) as a favour to its then-ally the Shah-ruled Iran; (2) as a ploy during the Cold War as Iraq was seen as an ally of the Soviet Union; (3) as a means to relieve pressure on Israel so that Iraq would not join some future Arab attack on the Jewish state; and (4) as a means to possibly satisfy its own need for Middle East oil, since Barzani had promised that the United States could look to a friend in OPEC once oil-rich Kurdistan had achieved independence.

Accordingly, President Richard Nixon and his national security adviser and later secretary of state Henry Kissinger first encouraged the Iraqi Kurds to revolt against Baghdad, but then with their ally Iran double-crossed the Kurds when the Shah decided to make a deal with Saddam Hussein. To rationalise US actions, Kissinger argued that the 'benefit of Nixon's Kurdish decision was apparent in just over a year: Only one Iraqi division was available to participate in the October 1973 Middle East

War.'[11] Cynically, he also declaimed that 'covert action should not be confused with missionary work.'[12]

Barzani himself died a broken man four years later in US exile as an unwanted ward of the CIA.[13] Years later Jonathan Randal argued that Barzani's son and eventual successor Massoud Barzani had 'never forgotten Kissinger's treachery in 1975, had never totally recovered from the humiliation of his years of enforced exile, which he blamed on the United States [...] [and] never stopped worrying about American constancy.'[14] Massoud Barzani himself explained that 'we have had bitter experience with the US government [...] In 1975 [...] it changed its alliances purely in its own interest at the expense of our people's suffering and plight.'[15]

More than a quarter of a century later, Kissinger revisited what the United States had done under his stewardship and explained that 'saving the [Iraqi] Kurds [in 1975] would have required the opening of a new front in inhospitable mountains close to the Soviet border.'[16] Thus, 'we did not have the option of overt support in a war so logistically difficult, so remote, and so incomprehensible to the American public.' Moreover, 'the Shah had made the decision, and we had neither the plausible arguments nor strategies to dissuade him.' Kissinger then concluded, 'As a case study, the Kurdish tragedy provides material for a variety of conclusions: the need to clarify objectives at the outset; the importance of relating goals to available means; the need to review an operation periodically; and the importance of coherence among allies.' In other words the Iraqi Kurds had played the role of dispensable pawns for American foreign policy.

Third stage

The third stage of American foreign policy towards the Kurds began with the Gulf War in 1991 and lasted until the US attack on Iraq in March 2003. This third stage led to the creation of the KRG, the closest approximation of an independent Kurdish state in modern times. As the Iraqi military was being ousted from Kuwait, President George H. W. Bush encouraged 'the Iraqi people to take matters into their own hands—to force Saddam Hussein, the dictator, to step aside.'[17] Despite initial successes, however, neither the Iraqi Shiites nor the Kurds proved able to cope with Saddam Hussein's stronger military. As Saddam Hussein began to put the Kurdish rebellion down, the two Iraqi Kurdish leaders—Massoud Barzani of the KDP and Jalal Talabani of the PUK—appealed to Bush for help by reminding him, 'You personally called upon the Iraqi people to rise up against Saddam Hussein's brutal dictatorship.'[18]

For a variety of reasons, however, the United States decided not to intervene in the internal Iraqi strife. Doing so could lead, it was feared, to an unwanted, protracted US occupation that would be politically unpopular in the United States, to an unstable government in Iraq, or even to 'Lebanonization' of the country and destabilisation of the Middle East. Furthermore, the United States also concluded that Saddam Hussein could win. To support the Kurds against him might require an unwanted, permanent American commitment. Possibly too, the memory of America overreaching itself in the Korean War, by trying to totally replace the North Korean regime after initially liberating South Korea, also influenced US thinking. In addition, Kurdish success in Iraq might provoke Kurdish uprisings in Turkey, Syria or Iran, states whose co-operation the United States felt it needed. (All of these problems, of course, came back to haunt the United States after its second war against Saddam Hussein in 2003 under the second President Bush.) A US Senate Foreign Relations staff report written by Peter Galbraith and issued a month after Saddam Hussein had put down the rebellion confirmed that the United States 'continued to see the opposition in caricature' and feared that the Kurds would seek a separate state and that the Shiites wanted an Iranian-style republic.[19]

Once it became clear the United States was not going to intervene in 1991, the uneven struggle turned into a rout and some 1.5 million Kurdish refugees fled to the Iranian and Turkish frontiers where they faced death from the hostile climate and lack of provisions. This refugee dilemma quickly created a disastrous political problem for everyone involved, including the United States, Turkey and Iran. Thus, after much soul searching, the United States reversed itself and took several steps to protect the Kurds. United Nations Security Council Resolution 688 of 5 April 1991 condemned 'the repression of the Iraqi civilian population […] in Kurdish populated areas' and demanded 'that Iraq […] immediately end this repression'. Under the aegis of Operation Provide Comfort (OPC) and a no-fly zone imposed against Baghdad, the Kurds were able to return to their homes in northern Iraq where they began to build a fledgling de facto state and government, which soon became today's KRG. (The current Syrian refugee problem—which involves a substantial number of Syrian Kurds—is an eerie reminder of this earlier tragedy.)

The continuance of OPC became a major political issue in Turkey, however, because many Turks believed it was facilitating the vacuum of authority in northern Iraq that enabled the PKK to enjoy sanctuaries there. Some even argued that OPC was the opening salvo of a new Treaty of Sèvres (1920) that would lead to the creation of a Kurdish state in northern Iraq as almost occurred following the First World War. Thus, went the argument, Turkey was facilitating its own demise by backing OPC. (This argument, of course, became even more relevant during the next stage of American foreign policy towards the Kurds that began in 2003.)

To abandon OPC, however, would alienate Washington and strip Ankara of important influence over the course of events. OPC, for example, enabled Turkey to launch military strikes into Iraqi Kurdistan against the PKK at almost any time. If the United States refused to allow such Turkish incursions, Turkey could threaten to withdraw its permission for OPC. Although it might have seemed ironic that an operation that was supposed to protect the Iraqi Kurds was allowing Turkey to attack the Turkish Kurds as well as inflicting collateral damage on the host Iraqi Kurds, such was the logic of the Kurdish imbroglio and part of the dilemma for America foreign policy. Similar dilemmas exist for the United States today concerning Syria as support for the opposition would involve al-Qaeda-affiliated groups that are also fighting against the Syrian Kurds. However, US support for the PYD, which is the strongest Syrian Kurdish party, would be for a group affiliated with the PKK, which the United States deems a terrorist organisation.

Moreover, in May 1994, the two main Iraqi Kurdish parties—the KDP and the PUK—fell into a civil war that immensely complicated American foreign policy towards them. How could the United States help and protect the Iraqi Kurds when they were busy killing themselves? In late January 1995, President Bill Clinton sent a message to both Barzani and Talabani in which he warned, 'We will no longer co-operate with the other countries to maintain security in the region if the clashes continue.'[20]

The situation was then allowed to drift with the United States declining to try harder to effect a ceasefire between the Iraqi Kurds or to contribute a mere $2 million to an international mediation force that might have forestalled the next round of fighting.[21] In August 1996, a sudden renewal of the intra-Kurdish struggle seemed likely to result in a PUK victory, given the arms it had received from Iran. Desperate, Barzani did the unthinkable and invited Saddam Hussein in to help him against Talabani.

How could the United States enforce the no-fly zone against Saddam Hussein when the very people it was supposed to be protecting had invited Saddam Hussein in? Halfheartedly, the United States responded by bombing a few meaningless targets south of Baghdad. Saddam Hussein used the few hours he had to capture and execute some ninety-six Iraqis who had defected to the US-financed Iraqi opposition, the Iraqi National Congress (INC). A senior INC official claimed, 'in two hours, the Iraqi opposition [had] lost its entire infrastructure',[22] while a US official concluded, 'our entire covert program has gone to hell'.[23]

New peace initiatives early the next year, however, finally led to significant developments and renewed attempts by the United States to bring the Iraqi Kurds together. Following a successful high-level meeting at the end of August 1998 between KDP officials and Talabani, in early September 1998 first Barzani and then Talabani journeyed to Washington. After separate individual meetings with US State Department officials, the two Iraqi Kurdish leaders finally met personally for the first time since the summer of 1994, when their civil war had begun. After two days of lengthy sessions, they reached a tentative agreement to permanently end their fighting and establish peace.

In announcing this pact, US Secretary of State Madeleine Albright also made general promises of American support for the Iraqi Kurds—contingent upon their continuing unity—by declaring, 'the United States will decide how and when to respond to Baghdad's actions based on the threat they pose to Iraq's neighbors, to regional security, to vital US interests and to the Iraqi people, including those in the north.'[24] President Clinton repeated Albright's lukewarm assurances in letters to Congress on 6 November 1998 and again on 19 May 1999.[25] Although these pronouncements did not constitute an ironclad agreement of protection, they were—in contrast to Nixon's and Kissinger's covert and unkept promises of a quarter of a century earlier—public declarations. Thus, they could not be and have not been so cavalierly ignored, particularly after the Iraqi Kurds supported the United States in its war to overthrow Saddam Hussein in 2003. Subsequently, of course, the United States has had to walk a fine line as mediator between the new Baghdad government and the KRG, both of which it largely created. The United States also walks a potentially delicate line in Syria today by trying to give nuanced support to opposition that will not benefit al-Qaeda-affiliated groups covertly supported by US ally Turkey. The latter seeks to restrain by these means the Syrian Kurds who, however, are largely secular and pro-Western. Would Solomon himself know how to respond?

Fourth stage

The fourth stage of American foreign policy towards the Kurds began with the US war to remove Saddam Hussein from power in March 2003 and continues to the present (2013). This most recent period might also be called the de facto US-KRG alliance stage. Until this fourth stage, Turkey's opposition to Kurdish identity, and Turkey's strongest strategic alliance with the United States since the days of the Truman Doctrine first promulgated in 1947, had arguably been two of the main reasons for the inability of the Kurds to create any type of independent state in the modern Middle East that began to develop after the First World War. Although the United States had always paid lip service to the idea of Kurdish rights, whenever it was necessary to make a choice, the United States always backed its strategic NATO ally Turkey when it came to the Kurdish issue.

Only when the United States perceived the Iraqi Kurds to be a useful foil against Saddam Hussein did Washington begin to take a partially pro-Kurdish position, at least towards the Iraqi Kurds. However, this US support for the Iraqi Kurds did not prohibit Turkey from unilaterally intervening in northern Iraq in pursuit of the PKK during the 1980s and 1990s. However, US support for the developing KRG, the disagreements over sanctions against Saddam Hussein's Iraq and problems over the future of Iraq itself gradually helped begin to fray the longstanding US-Turkish alliance.

The US war to remove Saddam Hussein from power in 2003 furthered this process and even partially reversed alliance partners. For the first time since the creation of Iraq, the Iraqi Kurds now had a powerful ally in the United States. This ironic situation was brought about by Turkey refusing to allow the United States to use its territory as a base for a northern front to attack Saddam Hussein's Iraq in March 2003 during the second Gulf War. Courtesy of Turkey, the Iraqi Kurds were suddenly thrust into the role of US ally, a novel position they eagerly and successfully assumed. Quickly, the Iraqi Kurds occupied the oil-rich Kirkuk and

Mosul areas, which would have been unthinkable encroachments upon Turkish red lines had Turkey anchored the northern front. What is more, Turkey had no choice but to acquiesce in the Iraqi Kurdish moves.

The new situation was further illustrated in July 2003 when the United States apprehended eleven Turkish commandos in the Iraqi Kurdish city of Sulaymaniya who were apparently seeking to carry out acts intended to destabilise the de facto Kurdish government and state in northern Iraq. Previously, as the strategic ally of the United States, Turkey had had *carte blanche* to do practically anything it wanted in northern Iraq. No longer was this true. The 'Sulaymaniya incident' caused what one high-ranking Turkish general called the 'worst crisis of confidence'[26] in US-Turkish relations since the creation of the NATO alliance. It also illustrated how the United States was willing to protect the Iraqi Kurds from unwanted Turkish interference. What is more, Washington now began to reject Turkish proposals that the United States should either eliminate the PKK guerrillas holed up in northern Iraq or permit the Turkish army to do so. Previously, the Turkish army had entered northern Iraq any time it desired in pursuit of the PKK.

Accordingly, many observers now stress how the Iraqi Kurds love the Americans. Yes, but. Although the United States is currently widely popular in the KRG, it is with a background caveat reminding all that they were betrayed twice before by the United States: in 1975 and again in 1991, as mentioned above. Indeed, as already mentioned, some Kurds began to fear the worst when the Iraq Study Group Report—co-authored by former US Secretary of State James A. Baker III and the former US Congressman Lee H. Hamilton and released in December 2006—suggested that the hard-won KRG federal state might have to be sacrificed to the perceived need for a re-established centralised Iraqi state.[27] Fortunately, for the KRG, President George W. Bush did not adopt these recommendations, but their mere broaching showed how tenuous future US support might be.

Nevertheless, the KRG leadership maintains that it received renewed US guarantees of protection in December 2009. At a meeting in Irbil between the KRG President Massoud Barzani and US Secretary of Defense Robert Gates, the latter assured the Iraqi Kurds by declaring, 'We recognize the concerns that you have about the future of your people and we will help you to ensure a prosperous and peaceful Iraq. We will not abandon you.'[28] In addition, Gates made the following three commitments: '(1) To use our influence to ensure that the outstanding disputes between the KRG and the Iraqi Government, including the Kirkuk dispute and other disputed areas and the sharing of oil revenues, are resolved based on the Iraqi Constitution and Article 140 regarding the future of Kirkuk. (2) To continue with our military efforts with the Peshmerga (KRG defense forces) as well as with the Iraqi Army and security forces within the framework of our joint security architecture. (3) To offer our support and assistance for a census to be conducted in Iraq next year.'[29]

A few days later, the Obama administration gave the Iraqi Kurds what they maintained was a 'historic'[30] commitment when it promised to broker disputes between them and the Baghdad government as well as giving support in resolving the vexed issue of Kirkuk.[31] This US support was in return for the Iraqi Kurds agreeing to accept a new election law that would give them a few less seats in the new Iraqi parliament that was elected on 7 March 2010. The delicate Baghdad-Irbil balance has continued despite the US troop withdrawal from Iraq at the end of 2011. This has required the KRG leadership to practise particularly astute diplomacy to survive.

The fifth (PKK) stage

Commencing a decade earlier, and then overlapping the third and fourth stages analysed above, is what might be called the fifth or PKK stage of American foreign policy towards the Kurds. In contrast to its support for the 'good' Iraqi Kurds and despite Turkish conspiracy theories to the contrary,[32] the United States has very strongly opposed the 'bad' Kurds of the PKK. Turkey's longtime and continuing geostrategically important position as a US–NATO ally is clearly the main reason for this situation. Other explanations include the US fear of Islamic extremism and Turkey's alliance with Israel, which, however is currently on hold. As a constitutionally secular state, Turkey is seen as a bastion against Islamic extremism, while support for Israel remains a given for American foreign policy.

Although it continues to criticise Turkey in its annual human rights country reports,[33] the United States has also maintained that the PKK are 'terrorists' who 'frequently kill noncombatants, and target village officials, village guards, teachers and other perceived representatives of the state'.[34] 'The PKK are terrorists. Turkey is going after terrorists. The PKK are indiscriminately killing their own people. They are not supported by the majority of Kurds.'[35] Other US officials claim that they have compiled a thick dossier on the PKK that includes murder, drug trafficking, extortion, robbery and trafficking in illegal immigrants.[36] The US State Department has also long had the PKK on its list of terrorist organisations, but never the KDP or PUK of the Iraqi Kurds.

US support for Turkey on the Kurdish issue was amply illustrated by the help it gave Turkey to capture Abdullah Ocalan, the leader of the PKK. When Turkey forced Syria to finally expel Ocalan from his long-time sanctuary in that country in October 1998, the United States backed Turkey by sending a strongly worded letter to Syria regarding the situation.[37] After a short, surreptitious stay in Russia, Ocalan arrived in Italy where for a brief period it looked like he might be able to turn his military defeat into a political victory by having the EU try him and thus also try Turkey.

Although the Italians and other Europeans such as the Germans initially appeared sympathetic, at this point the United States weighed in heavily by denouncing Ocalan in the strongest of terms as a terrorist. The United States also pressured Italy—and any other state tempted to offer the PKK leader asylum and a platform from which to negotiate—to instead extradite him to Turkey for trial. An editorial from the US State Department broadcast by the Voice of America declared, 'It is neither US practice nor policy to provide an international platform from which terrorists can expound their views or try to justify their criminal actions. No one should doubt our views on Ocalan; the United States considers him a terrorist who should be brought to justice for his crimes.'[38]

As he flew from country to country, James Foley, the State Department representative, seemingly mocked Ocalan by joking, 'I'd hate to be the pilot of that small plane.'[39] Desperate, Ocalan finally allowed the Greeks to take him to their embassy in Nairobi, Kenya where US intelligence agents had inundated the country following the US embassy bombing there the previous summer. At this point American animus towards the PKK leader entered its final stage by providing Turkey with the technical intelligence to pinpoint his whereabouts and capture him. Mark Parris, the US ambassador to Turkey, approvingly spoke of 'Ocalan's rendition',[40] an archaic term referring to the surrender of a fugitive slave.

Although the US war to overthrow Saddam Hussein in 2003 brought new tensions between the United States and Turkey over the Kurdish issue, more recently the United States has continued to support its long-time Turkish ally against the PKK now ensconced in the Qandil mountains of the KRG. Late in 2007, for example, the United States began giving Turkey 'actionable intelligence'[41] on the PKK's location. Then in February 2008, Turkey, armed with this intelligence, launched its first military incursion into northern Iraq against the PKK since the 1990s. As in earlier times, the United States did not object despite its de facto alliance with the KRG. In February 2010, US Secretary of Defense Robert Gates indicated that the United States was seeking to determine whether it could offer Turkey even more help with equipment and intelligence to combat the PKK.[42] Moreover, when Turkey finally began negotiating with the PKK early in 2013, the United States proved pleased to support their peace process. Turkey's much greater gravitas and value as a US ally had inevitably been reasserted.

The sixth (Syrian) stage

The sixth or Syrian stage of American foreign policy towards the Kurds stems from the Syrian civil war. The United States had long viewed Syria with caution and often hostility as a radical Arab state sponsor of international terrorism and an implacable foe of Israel. This position was formalised by the Syria Accountability and Lebanese Sovereignty Restoration Act (SALSRA) that Congress passed on 12 December 2003. The stated purpose of this bill was to end what the United States saw as Syria's support for terrorism and illegal presence in Lebanon, stop Syria's development of weapons of mass destruction which included chemical weapons, and halt Syria's illegal importation of Iraqi oil and shipments of military items to anti-US forces in Iraq. Ironically, however, SALSRA did not address Syrian violation of human rights

At the time of writing in October 2013, the United States had the following priorities in Syria: 1) Respond successfully to the regime's probable chemical attack against elements of the opposition on 21 August 2013; 2) Protect Israel; 3) Oppose Iran; 4) Curb al-Qaeda; 5) Maintain Syrian unity.[43] All five of these last goals could be vitiated if a successful solution to the first one was not found.

On 21 August 2013 the Syrian regime apparently used chemical weapons against the opposition in Ghouta, an eastern suburb of Damascus, killing anywhere from 500 to 1,400 people—the numbers vary according to US intelligence reports made public. While the Assad regime had long had a great deal of innocent blood on its hand and now probably was guilty of using chemical weapons, this was not a sufficient reason for the United States and its Western allies to bomb Syria. Indeed, the United States had neither an intelligent entry plan nor an exit plan if it did so.

In the first place, however, it was not yet even certain the Syrian regime actually used these weapons. US intelligence on these matters has erred and lied to the world before. For example, in 1998 the United States bombed a pharmaceutical plant in Sudan claiming that Sudan had supplied al-Qaeda with chemical weapons that had been used in its attacks on US embassies in Kenya and Tanzania. Later, however, it learned that the intelligence supposedly implicating Sudan was incorrect. Similarly in the run-up to the war that toppled Saddam Hussein in 2003, a war whose slaughter and repercussions are still being felt a decade later, the United States falsely claimed that it had incontrovertible intelligence that Iraq possessed weapons of mass destruction, which justified attacking. It turned out that US intelligence was wrong again or had simply lied to justify going to war.

Given such an uncertain track record, why should we be so certain that the US intelligence was correct this time? And even if it were correct, did this justify bombing just because the Syrian regime had crossed a red line drawn by the United States, which then would lose face if it did not retaliate? Furthermore, some have even claimed that the Syrian opposition was the real culprit because it wanted to get the United States to topple the Assad regime, which it could not do itself. As both the United Nations and Russia demanded, positive proof was called for before one could expect the international community to go down this road again.

The United States justified its possible attack against Syria on the grounds that the Assad regime has violated international law by using chemical weapons. However, using napalm in Vietnam had not bothered the United States when it was the one using such weapons. More recently, the United States simply ignored Saddam Hussein's use of chemical weapons against the Kurds in Halabja on 16 March 1988 because in those days Saddam was its ally. Does anyone believe that the United States would have made all this fuss about chemical weapons if it had been the opposition in Syria that had used them?

It is patently illegal under international law for the United States to bomb Syria unless authorised to do so by the United Nations Security Council or in immediate self-defence. Neither applied to the situation in hand. The legal way for the United States to respond to this crisis was to negotiate with Russia to bring the Security Council on board. After all, the United Nations was constituted in the first place not to take military action unless all five permanent members of the Security Council concurred. Otherwise, the United Nations would simply become the tool of one great power or the other, not the arm of international peace and cooperation. One might argue that the United Nations' inaction in this case was the wiser course, although President Obama and his supporters initially did not want to hear this. Barring UN action, the United States might have sought Arab League support. However, by bombing without such international approval, the United States would be violating international law.

Furthermore, a bombing campaign by the United States would run the risk of escalating the Syrian civil war into a regional and even international war that might involve Russia and Iran and inevitably bring in Israel. Despite assurances that it would only conduct precise surgical strikes, the resulting 'collateral damage' that would inevitably kill innocent civilians if the United States bombed Syria was yet another reason not to pursue bombing as a course of action. What is more, the Assad regime would surely have sought to retaliate in some way if bombed. Tit-for-tat bombings could soon escalate into a much larger war.

In addition, if the United States succeeded in bombing Assad into surrender, it might lead to an even worse situation from the point of view of the US national interest, because some of the most powerful elements of the Syrian opposition, as noted above, are affiliated with al-Qaeda, Jabhat al-Nusra and the Islamic State of Iraq and al-Sham (ISIS), for example. US action against Assad could bring about the law of unintended consequences. If a small al-Qaeda-run state actually came to power in a post-Assad splintered Syria, suddenly the United States would have to exercise real self-defence against Syria. The KRG in Iraq would also want to avoid an al-Qaeda statelet as a neighbour.

Furthermore, if the United States with British or French allies struck Syria, it would have looked like Western imperialism again rearing its ugly head in the Middle East. More unwanted blowback from a union of Arab nationalists with Islamic jihadists and Salafists would probably be the result.

The major problem for the United States was that it had not offered any valid strategy for what it would be trying to accomplish by bombing Syria, other than somehow supposedly punishing the Assad regime for using chemical weapons. Obama has already ruled out regime change. But without really degrading Assad's assets, pinprick US attack would do little but arouse his anger and determination to fight on and even retaliate against the United States and its regional partners.

In the end, the British Parliament took the almost unprecedented decision to vote down a prime minister's motion to go to war, thereby inhibiting the freedom of action the US might otherwise have enjoyed. President Obama reacted quickly, throwing the decision into the hands of the US Congress, thereby salvaging a modicum of credibility and earning the opportunity to share the blame if any bombing backfired. In the short run, this would be good for the president and the United States.

However, in letting Congress make the final decision, Obama was setting a dangerous precedent in appearing to share the power to decide on war and peace, which was one of his greatest assets. He might soon regret this loss of power as the spectre of Iran's nuclear weapons programme loomed in the near future, despite similar warnings about red lines, and posed a much more serious threat to US national security than Syria's use of chemical weapons. North Korea's nuclear ambitions offered similar problems. Egypt's new military regime also continued to ignore US calls for peace after killing more than 600 protesters. Iraq's continuing sectarian killings and Afghanistan's shaky future once US troops pull out in 2014 also represent potentially messy problems for the United States in the near future for which the president might want the authority to move quickly without Congressional deliberation and approval.

As for protecting Israel, bombing Syria to punish Assad might cause him to retaliate against Israel as Saddam Hussein did in 1991 when he came under US attack. Israel, of course, can take care of itself, but any time the Jewish state comes under attack from an Arab opponent there is the immediate risk of an all-out regional war or worse. Thus, protecting Israel might best be done by not bombing Syria.

Similarly, for opposing Iran, curbing al-Qaeda and even maintaining Syria's unity, US bombing might force Iran's hand to more overtly defend its all-important and only Arab ally, Assad. On the other hand, it might also be true that doing nothing about Assad's probable use of chemical weapons might lead Iran to conclude that the United States would do nothing seriously about Iran building nuclear weapons.

Furthermore, if US bombing led to Assad's overthrow, such al-Qaeda-affiliated groups as Jabhat al-Nusra and the ISIS, among others, might have a better chance to craft some sort of long-term institutional power out of the ruins of a splintered Syria. Again, bombing Syria in retaliation for its probable use of chemical weapons might work against all five of the US priorities listed above in that beleaguered state.

Finally, there were of course other options. Covert operations famously reinstated the US-friendly Shah of Iran in 1953 and even earlier supported Husni Zaim's military coup in Syria in 1949, overthrew the supposedly pro-communist Arbenz regime in Guatemala in 1954 and had a hand in who knows what else over the years. Similarly, clandestine actions might be able to accomplish whatever the United States felt it had to do in Syria without risking as much blowback.[44] Arming selected opposition groups that were secularly inclined, tougher smart sanctions, encouraging more defections from Assad's entourage, and more vigorous diplomacy to bring Russia on board were all possibilities that needed to be examined.

In the event, the United States apparently found a way out of its chemical weapons dilemma in Syria, by taking up Russia's suggestion that Assad should surrender his arsenal to international control and destruction. Although many in the United States and the Syrian opposition criticised Obama's UN option as feckless, the UN route not only avoided most of the pitfalls of the United States unilaterally bombing Syria, but also provided a legal diplomatic strategy. Only time, of course, would tell how successful this action would prove. By this time the United Nations had issued its report on the chemical weapons attack. While it did not specifically state that the Assad regime was guilty, the report largely implicated it by the rockets and launchers used, as well as the direction from which they had been launched.

On the other hand, by opposing Kurdish autonomy in Syria as leading to secessionism and to please its NATO ally Turkey, the United

States might find itself weakening a secular Kurdish ally that was successfully combating al-Qaeda-affiliated enemies of the United States. This was the case at the time of writing since the United States had hesitated to give heavy military equipment to the opposition, fearing that it would fall into anti-Western, jihadist/Salafist hands.

In July 2013, however, the United States saw fit to denounce the PKK-affiliated PYD for clashes in the town of Amuda in which the PYD had killed several Kurds from other parties. Once again, by denouncing the strongest Kurdish party battling the Salafists, the United States ironically was implicitly supporting al-Qaeda. The PYD itself replied that it had to defend itself against the al-Qaeda-affiliated al-Nursa brigade.[45] Probably in deference to its Turkish ally, the United States has also opposed the PYD's plans to establish some kind of Kurdish administration in the areas of Syria they now dominate.

However, the PYD claims it has been in hopeful contact with the United States over the issue.[46] Indeed, Salih Muslim has appealed to both the United States and Europe to support the Kurds against their common al-Qaeda-affiliated enemy in the Syrian civil war.[47] 'I want the American public and the entire world to know that we are trying to stop these jihadist groups, and we want them to stand with us. These people attack innocent civilians and kill children, women and old people simply because they are Kurds.' The PYD leader furthered claimed that the jihadists 'issue fatwas that raping Kurdish women and looting their properties is legitimate, after you kill their husbands' and added that 'this is what happened in Tal Abyad recently […] [and in] the Tal Arn and Tal Hasel towns of Aleppo.'

Continuing, Salih Muslim asserted that, 'unfortunately, the United States and Europe have not done anything yet […] [and] have not even condemned atrocities against civilian Kurds […] They do not even send us humanitarian aid!' Salih Muslim went on to complain that 'everybody in Syria received international aid, but not us, the Kurds! On the contrary, we are under an embargo from all around.' The PYD leader added that, 'I have applied twice for a visa to travel to the United States, but they did yet not respond to my request.' He also said, 'I do not know either why American officials are not willing to meet with us', and declared that, 'we have never had any animosity against America and the American people.' Warming to his task, Salih Muslim even proclaimed that 'we see our future in Western democracy' because 'the United States is the cradle of democracy and the American people support freedom for everyone [...] There is no doubt that the interests of the American people are not contrary to ours.' The Syrian civil war—which of course permeates any discussion of the Kurds in Syria—will be discussed at greater length in a subsequent chapter.

8

PRELUDE

In addition to the Syrian civil war which broke out in March 2011, two other events served as catalysts or as preludes to the unexpected autonomy that suddenly was thrust upon the Kurds in Syria on 19 July 2012: the Qamishli uprising (*Serhildan*) in March 2004 and the assassination of Mishaal Tammo on 7 October 2011.

*The Qamishli uprising (*Serhildan*)*

On 12 March 2004, a riot broke out at a football match in Qamishli between fans of the local Kurdish team and Sunni Arab fans of the opposing team from Dayr al-Zur to the south, eventually leading to further demonstrations throughout Kurdish areas of the country including the Kurdish quarters of Hama, Aleppo and Damascus. Rioters destroyed statues of Hafez al-Assad as well as a number of government structures, and the security forces responded by killing at first six Kurds and eventually as many as thirty to fifty others, while arresting more than 2,000. Hundreds of others were injured.

On the second day, Qamishli witnessed thousands of people turning out for the procession to the cemetery where the six victims of the first day of riots were buried. Security forces again fired into the crowd, which led to Kurdish attacks against government buildings, the railway station and the toppling of Hafez al-Assad's statues. The latter action was a powerful symbolic act against the regime reminiscent of what had happened to the statue of Saddam Hussein in Baghdad less than one year earlier, as well as a strong statement in a state where the ruling family was supposed to be inviolable. Word quickly spread to other Kurdish communities in Syria including Kurdish quarters in the major cities via cell phones, and the riots escalated.

These unprecedented demonstrations and riots were not planned by the Kurdish parties, which feared a backlash and counselled restraint,[1] but were spontaneous popular outbursts that continued until 25 March when the regime's forces finally prevailed. However, the *Serhildan* still led to a newly found Kurdish self-awareness and pride that marked a definite turning point in the Kurdish existence within Syria and was, therefore, a momentous event around which the Kurds could subsequently rally. For the first time in the history of the Kurds in Syria, a protest movement had united all the Kurds as well as eliciting support from the Kurds in Turkey and Iraq. Indeed, one year later, as mentioned above, Massoud Barzani, the president of the KRG, called upon the Syrian government to grant the Kurds in Syria their democratic rights, a first for him given the implicit understanding that forbade foreign Kurdish criticism of Damascus in return for sanctuary.

The Kurdish term *serhildan* illustrated this new situation as it never before had been applied to Syria. The word is made up of two shorter ones, *ser* (head) and *hildan* (to raise or to lift up). The resulting compound term means in Kurdish (Kurmanji) rebellion, revolt or insurrection. Before Qamishli, the Kurds in Syria had only used the word for the Kurdish protests in Turkey in March 1990 and the uprising that occurred in Iraq in 1991. The PKK also had used the word following the arrest of Abdullah Ocalan in 1999 and for subsequent events in Turkey during 2005 and 2008. The term *serhildan* also suggests a genuinely popular movement of an oppressed people and is similar to the Arabic word *intifada* used to describe popular Palestinian uprisings against Israel. (Many Kurds, however, are not so sympathetic to Arab calls to support the Palestinian cause since most Arabs deny the legitimacy of the Kurdish cause.) Earlier Sivan Perwer, the famous Kurdish singer, had also popularised the term with his song *Serhildan Jiyan e'* (Uprising is life) about the Iraqi chemical attack on the Kurdish city of Halabja on 16 March 1988.

According to Kurdish sources, the supporters of the visiting Sunni Arab team started the initial riots by chanting insults against the Iraqi Kurdish leaders Barzani and Talabani, while flaunting portraits of Saddam Hussein. Kurdish fans responded by chanting praises of US President George W. Bush. Arab supporters used knives, stones and sticks, thus escalating the clashes onto the streets of Qamishli.

However, other sources claimed that at a match in Dayr al-Zur two weeks earlier, some Kurdish fans had provoked the Sunni Arab fans by cursing Saddam Hussein and showing support for the recently promulgated Transnational Administrative Law or draft constitution for post-Saddam Iraq that formally recognised the KRG. In addition, Newroz, the Kurdish New Year's Day celebration, also falls in March and often acts as a catalyst for protests. Further reports indicated, therefore, that the regime was in a state of high alert and had mobilised security forces. If so, however, why did the state then allow the second football match in Qamishli even to be held?

In June 2005, yet another event galvanised the Kurds in Syria and led to further demonstrations: the disappearance and murder of Sheikh Maashouq Khaznawi. Khaznawi was a Kurdish Sufi leader who had demanded justice and political reform for the Kurds. Although the regime claimed he had been killed by a criminal gang, many Kurds believed that the state had perpetrated the deed. Large demonstrations consisting of as many as 25,000 people chanting slogans for Kurdish autonomy were held at his funeral in Qamishli, resulting in the security forces killing several more protesters. Sheikh Khaznawi quickly became a new iconic symbol of martyrdom in the emerging Syrian Kurdish nationalist narrative. The prelude was set for a more powerful and emboldened Kurdish identity and initiatives.

The Syrian civil war

It is difficult to write conclusively about an ongoing event such as the Syrian civil war. This, however, has not deterred a number of scholars.[2] The Syrian civil war began in March 2011 as a struggle over socio-economic conditions and a fight for democracy, but quickly metastasised into a regional and even global proxy conflict.

Bashar al-Assad apparently believed the Syrian people valued stability instead of the chaos democracy had seemingly brought Iraq and Lebanon, that some of the opposition were asking too much too soon and that because he had opposed the war in Iraq in 2003, supported Lebanon's Hezbollah during its war against Israel in the summer of 2006 and Hamas against Israel when it invaded Gaza in December 2008, he would be protected from the Arab Spring popular revolts that began to sweep the Middle East in December 2010. However, these anti-Zionist and anti-imperialist credentials did not atone for the terrible socio-economic situation in Syria where a rapid birthrate combined with some 300,000 annual new entrants into the job market in which only 8,000 were finding meaningful employment. Badly managed attempts at reform had led to crony capitalism that rewarded merely the privileged and well-connected. Finally, the continuing state of martial law in effect for more than a half a century had suppressed democratic freedoms, while torture to control protests had become institutionalised.

When new opposition arose over the assassination of Lebanon's Rafiq Hariri in 2005, followed by Syria's forced exit from Lebanon, the Damascus Declaration of Syrian Oppositionists (October 2005) criticised the regime's Lebanon policies and called for a new social contract, pluralism, rule of law and a peaceful transfer of power. Then, when Vice President Abdul Halim Khaddam broke with Assad, accusing him of being involved in Hariri's assassination and allied with the reviving Muslim Brotherhood that the senior Assad had smashed in 1982, the regime reacted with a wave of new repression. Still the anti-Assad revolt did not have to occur if Assad had embraced the opposition and led reform towards more democracy. Instead the dictator concluded that the Tunisian and Egyptian dictators had fallen because they had not used enough force, that weakness had only encouraged their enemies and would encourage his. Then once the killings started, there was no turning back.

For its part the opposition was emboldened by the success of the Arab Spring in other countries and a desire to gain revenge for Hama in 1982. The Muslim Brotherhood, now once again part of the opposition, possessed money, cohesion and foreign allies in Egypt and Turkey. The resulting violence and deaths led each side to the security dilemma conclusion that it would only be safe if the other were eradicated. Thus, a popular uprising against a dictator had become entangled with a life or death domestic sectarian struggle that now raged between Sunnis and Alawites; a proxy regional conflict between Shiite Iran, Iraq and Hezbollah against Sunni Turkey, Saudi Arabia and Qatar; and on the international scene, a renewal of the Cold War struggle between the United States and its NATO allies against Russia and China. There was also an element of the absurd involved, with al-Qaeda affiliated groups such as Jabhat al-Nusra or Al-Nusra Front and the Islamic State of Iraq and Syria (ISIS)—

also known as Al-Qaeda of Iraq—supposed to be allied with the democratic Syrian opposition, thus enabling Assad and his supporters to be able to claim that they were defending secular values prized in the West against Islamic terrorist groups.

By September 2013, more than 100,000 persons had been killed, many more injured, more than 2 million had become refugees who had crossed the borders into Turkey, Lebanon, Jordan and Iraq, while within Syria there were at least 2 million Internally Displaced Persons, roughly 8 million more in need of humanitarian aid, and one-third of the housing stock damaged or destroyed.[3] By July 2013, according to one respected source, the Syrian economy had shrunk 35 per cent since the civil war had begun, unemployment had increased fivefold, the Syrian currency had decreased to one-sixth of its earlier value and the public sector had lost $15 billion.[4]

For a long time, it seemed to most observers that the Assad regime's days were numbered. After all, the Arab Spring had already washed away the dictators in Tunisia, Egypt and Libya. Practically every week seemed to bring new advances for the rebels to the extent that on 19 July 2012, the regime suddenly decided virtually to abandon the Kurdish areas of Syria in the north along the Turkish border in a desperate effort to consolidate and husband its remaining resources to retain what it still held. As we have already seen this decision enabled the Kurds to emerge out of nowhere and assume a de facto autonomy that will be analysed in the next chapter.

However, the viewpoint that the Assad regime was ready to collapse was probably misleading. For one thing, in contrast to the other regimes that had fallen, Damascus was able to mobilise civil servants, trade unionists, business groups, Islamists and other supporters such as Baath Party members as well as minorities and pro-regime nationalists. YouTube videos of victorious opposition fighters capturing military strong points and weapons gave the false impression that the regime was on the ropes. As the rebellion continues well into a third year, however, it has become clear that the reality is that no one is winning a quick victory. The Syrian civil war will more likely play out as did the extended civil war in Lebanon and the continuing fighting in Iraq.

How has the regime managed to hold on? Strong support from Iran, Hezbollah, Russia and to a lesser extent (now Shiite) Iraq is probably the main factor, especially when countered against the lesser support, especially in troops and heavy equipment, that the opposition has been receiving from the United States and its NATO allies and Qatar, Saudi Arabia and the United Arab Emirates.

Iran has been key to the regime's survival. The two have had a strategic alliance since the Islamic Republic first came to power. As soon as the Syrian civil war began, Iran sent arms, technical support and its Revolutionary Guards to protect its only Arab ally and also to keep supply lines open to its Shiite ally Hezbollah in neighbouring Lebanon.[5] Despite its own economic problems created by Western-imposed sanctions, Iran also granted Syria a $1 billion import credit line in January 2013. Iraq too has sent Shiite militants to help Assad, while also permitting Iranian planes to ship military supplies to Syria over Iraqi airspace.[6] The Iraqi foreign minister Hoshyar Zibari, who ironically happened to be a Kurd, said that there was nothing he could do to stop it. At the end of April 2013, Hassan Nasrallah, the leader of the powerful Shiite party/militia Hezbollah in Lebanon, reversed his earlier pronouncements on the subject and declared that his militia would aid Syria 'with its full organizational might' and would not allow it to 'fall into the hands of America, Israel or *takfiri* groups', the latter a reference to such al-Qaeda-affiliated Sunni fundamentalist organisations as al-Nusra.[7] A few months earlier, Hezbollah fighters had already helped to turn the tide of struggle for Qusayr, a town near the Lebanese-Syrian border some twenty miles south of Homs. Along with Iran, Hezbollah too has proven a staunch ally of the Assad regime.

Many feel that Russia has been Assad's greatest supporter.[8] Indeed, Russia has had a strong relationship with Syria since the 1950s. In 2010 Russian exports to Assad's regime were more than $1.1 billion, while its investments were almost $20 billion. Russia's only military base in the Mediterranean is at the Syrian port of Tartus. By supporting Syria, Russia also counters what it views as unrestricted United States/NATO influence in the Middle East. Therefore, on three occasions, Russia has used its veto in the UN Security Council to prevent an anti-Assad resolution. Some have also explained Russia's support as necessary to stop Islamist revolutions before they reach the Caucasus and other Muslim areas of Russia, which has already suffered greatly from past events in Chechnya.

Thus, Syria has obtained most of its military equipment such as tanks, missiles and anti-aircraft missile batteries from Russia. Russian suppliers have upgraded Syria's air defence systems since the civil war broke out and even manned some of them. In October 2012, Turkish authorities claimed that Russian munitions were discovered on a Syrian jet that had been forced to land in Ankara.[9]

In addition to Assad's foreign supporters, his opposition is fractured to the extent that some of its elements battle each other as well as Damascus. The so-called Free Syrian Army is nothing of the sort, merely a notional concept of several different, often conflicting, groups. The new National Coalition for Syrian Revolutionary and Opposition Forces that was created on 12 November 2012 in Doha, Qatar, has proved to be splintered as thoroughly as was the Syrian National Council (SNC) it replaced. When Moaz al-Khatib, the new Coalition's president, announced his willingness to meet Assad in February 2013, his hardline associates rejected his proposal even before the regime did: 'The opposition didn't even give us time to reject Moaz', joked a regime supporter.[10]

At times, the opposition has proved radical, criminal and even incompetent as well as riddled with fundamentalist groups openly allied with al-Qaeda. One YouTube video showed an opposition soldier eating the heart and liver of a dead Syrian army soldier, a disgusting act of cannibalism not well calculated to win over more moderate support such as the minorities and members of the urban elite who might have otherwise turned against the regime.[11] On 24 March al-Khatib, the moderate leader of the Syrian National Coalition, resigned declaring that since the Coalition was controlled by foreign powers such as Saudi Arabia and Qatar, it had lost the ability to decide for itself. His successor has had a similar lack of success.

What is more, the regime's strategy of pulling back from exposed outposts has enabled it to enjoy more defensible interior lines. Well into its third year, the opposition has been able to capture only one of sixteen provincial capitals: Raqqah in the east. In addition, with the counterinsurgency help of Hezbollah and Iranian advisers, the regime has restructured its forces by training a militia of 60,000 called the National Defence Force to protect positions that earlier tied down the regular army, which is now freed to launch counter-attacks. Basically, however, the regime is concentrating on retaining strategic areas and not trying to recapture the entire country and overwhelm the opposition, a task which appears to be well beyond its capacity.[12]

In addition, the opposition—which consists of a huge *lumpen* underclass that has been subjected to such extreme forms of regime violence that it believes (probably with good reason) that surrender would lead to its death—is not likely to give up short of suffering a total defeat and even then would probably continue the conflict on a lesser guerrilla level. Similarly, the regime's supporters also feel that it is either kill or be killed. Thus, it appears that the Syrian civil war will continue well into the future. If so, Syria is likely to descend into the ranks of failed states consisting of pockets of various embattled militias and statelets. And the longer this takes, the more likely Kurdish autonomy will become regularised and therefore institutionalised. However, before turning to this situation, one more prelude to it will be analysed.

Mishaal Tammo's assassination

As the civil war in Syria grew, Mishaal Tammo (1957–2011), the widely respected fifty-three-year-old leader (speaker) of the Syrian 'Kurdish Future Movement' and also a member of the executive committee of the what was then the recently formed, broadly-based opposition SNC, was assassinated in Qamishli in Syria on 7 October 2011. His wife and one of his six children were also injured in the attack. Tammo was attending a political meeting when the attack occurred. The assassination obviously held implications for the developing situation in Syria, especially the Kurds. Who was responsible and why did they do it? What were the implications?

Syrian Kurdish groups blamed the Syrian government, as did Mahmoud Othman, a well-known Iraqi Kurdish political figure.[13] Syria, however, denied any involvement and blamed foreign interference, speculating that Turkey was behind the deed to encourage chaos which would trigger an armed Kurdish uprising that would topple the embattled Assad regime. Still others claimed that Iran was behind the assassination as a means of supporting its longtime ally Syria and also out of fear of its own restive Kurdish minority.

Only a month earlier, Mishaal Tammo had barely escaped an earlier attempt on his life and had since been in hiding. At that time, he specifically blamed the Syrian regime. Oddly enough, however, and illustrating the fractured condition of what is a group of at least twelve to fifteen separate Syrian Kurdish parties, Tammo also had stated that the earlier attempt on his life had been made by the PYD, the Syrian Kurdish group mentioned above and allied with the PKK of Turkey, but also reputed to be acting at times in concert with the Syrian regime. The motive for this and the second successful attempt was Tammo's opposition to the Syrian regime, which the PKK was seeking to court as a backup sanctuary if its guerrillas were to be pushed out of the rugged Qandil mountains of Iraqi Kurdistan. The PYD had also been accused of the assassination because of competing attempts at holding demonstrations.[14] Indeed, subsequent violence broke out between the PYD and Kurdish National Council (KNC), a loose alliance of most of the other Syrian Kurdish political parties.[15] Tammo, however, had also made it clear that he believed it was the Syrian regime that was behind the PYD's actions.

Following Tammo's assassination, 50,000 demonstrators took to the streets in Qamishli for his funeral. It was maybe the largest demonstration in the Kurdish areas since the Arab Spring uprising against Assad had begun in March 2011. Security forces killed six of them. Other large demonstrations took place in the suburbs of Aleppo, Latakia and Hasaka. Smaller protests were held before the Syrian embassies in Berlin, Vienna and London, and Syria's permanent mission to the United Nations in Geneva. Other protests in sympathy for Tammo were staged in Britain, France and the Netherlands, leading to speculation that a real turning point had been reached in favour of Kurdish unity in Syria and support for the uprising against the regime. Ironically, therefore, the embattled Assad government had only recently rescinded the notorious Decree 93 passed in 1962 which had denied citizenship to some 120,000 Kurdish *ajanib* and another 75,000 Syrian Kurds known as *maktoumeen*. As the famous French scholar Alexis de Tocqueville once observed: revolutions seldom start when things are at their worst, but rather when they are getting better.

By the summer of 2011, Turkey had broken with Assad over his bloody repression. Turkey's new stance placed it into direct opposition to Iran, long Assad's ally. Thus, Iran saw Turkey's actions as a direct challenge to its interests. In addition, Turkey's actions in part could also be attributed to a desire to help shape events in its favour in a post-Assad Syria, unlike its failure to do so in post-Saddam Iraq where as a possible result a strong Kurdish movement had then arisen.

Until recently, Turkey had vehemently opposed Kurdish movements anywhere as a threat to its own existence. Recently, however, Turkish political policy has gradually altered with its economic interests in Iraqi Kurdistan and its own internal reforms driven in part by its EU accession hopes. Still, Turkey would at least want to inhibit any future Syrian Kurdish role in post-Assad Syria that might encourage Turkey's own embattled Kurds. On the issue of keeping the Syrian Kurds quiescent, Turkey would also be at odds with its nascent Iraqi Kurdish ally, the KRG in northern Iraq. Nevertheless, Turkey and the KRG have largely been able to work together regarding the Syrian Kurds.

In the event, Mishaal Tammo's assassination did not lead to immediate Syrian Kurdish unity, as such a thing would probably only occur as a gradual process. However, one still must conclude that his assassination served as a prelude that enabled the Kurds to seize the opportunity that was soon presented to them when the embattled Assad regime decided to precipitously pull its troops out of the Kurdish areas in the country's north in order better to defend what it still possessed to the south.

9

AUTONOMY

From being merely a sleepy unimportant backwater in the Kurdish strug-gle, Syria has suddenly graduated to being not only a burgeoning centre of newly empowered Kurdish nationalism, but even more important, a major flashpoint in the regional geopolitical situation. How did this occur?

As mentioned in the previous chapter, the Arab Spring revolt that broke out against the long-ruling Assad family in March 2011 quickly involved not only the many different groups within Syria, but also most of the surrounding states and parties, as each perceived the Syrian out-come as potentially bearing a most important impact on its own future. Turkey feared that the violence would spill over its borders[1] and further inflame its own Kurdish problems, especially as the PKK-affiliate PYD or Democratic Union Party headed by Salih Muslim (Mohammed) in Syria began to gain influence. The Syrian civil war was beginning to blur the border artificially dividing the Kurds since the end of the First World War.

To meet this threat, Turkey supported the opposition SNC, recreated after November 2012 as the National Coalition of Syrian Revolutionary and Opposition Forces or simply Syrian National Coalition. However, such Turkish support scared the Kurds in Syria away from backing the opposition as Turkey clearly had no interest in empowering the Syrian Kurds in a post-Assad Syria. The PYD especially argued this point. Fur-thermore, the Syrian Kurds did not trust any prospective Sunni Arab gov-ernment that might succeed Assad to grant or protect Kurdish rights. As Salih Muslim told this author, 'the mentality of Arabs cannot accept the

Kurds as a nation.'[2] For this reason most Kurdish parties including the PYD chose not to join either the SNC or its Coalition successor.

Shiite Iran, of course, felt its very future threatened if its main ally in the Middle East went down. Similarly, newly Shiite-ruled Iraq also felt a need to support Alawite-(a sect akin to the Shiites) ruled Syria. Lebanon's non-state, but still very influential (Shiite) Hezbollah also supported Assad. The Sunni-ruled KRG in Iraq, however, opposed Assad whose earlier anti-Kurdish record had been abysmal. The KRG's support for the Syrian opposition allied it with its new ally Turkey but against the PKK and its related Syrian affiliate the PYD, which in part implicitly supported Assad since they feared Turkish control of the Syrian opposition. Thus, even the Kurds in Syria were divided among themselves between the much stronger PYD and its various affiliates such as the People's Council of Western Kurdistan (PCWK) and the Kurdish National Council (KNC), which consisted of most of the other roughly twelve to fifteen Kurdish parties in Syria. Such Kurdish divisions in Syria, however, were not novel.

Nevertheless, in July 2012 KRG President Massoud Barzani managed to patch together a tenuous umbrella Supreme Kurdish Council out of the various Syrian Kurdish groups at a gathering held in Irbil. At the same time Barzani sought to further extend his influence among the Syrian Kurds by providing military training to some 600–2,000 who had fled to his jurisdiction from Syria.[3] Sunni-ruled states such as Saudi Arabia and Jordan also supported the Syrian opposition. As for Lebanon, the gallows humour had it that this notoriously divided state so closely connected to Syria was not being mentioned yet because it already had a bye into the final apocalypse. Israel, with an obvious interest in the Syrian outcome, probably also possessed a bye into the finals.

Outside the region, the United States and the EU cautiously supported the opposition, while Russia and China continued to support and even supply Assad because they did not want to set an unfortunate precedent for the international community to intervene in a state for human rights violations, which might come back to haunt them for their own misdeeds. Russia also supported Assad as a way of preventing perceived United States/NATO domination in the Middle East,[4] among other reasons discussed in the previous chapter. The result was that not only was international co-operation on what to do about the Syrian situation impossible to achieve, but even more the whole affair had the potential to escalate into a regional war.

With this incredibly complicated and evolving scenario in mind, this chapter will now turn to examine the sudden emergence of Salih Muslim and the PYD he led.

The rise of Salih Muslim and the PYD

Salih Muslim (born in 1951, married with five children, a chemical engineer and fluent in English) became active in the Kurdish movement during the 1970s while he was an engineering student at Istanbul Technical University and under the influence of Mulla Mustafa Barzani's revolt in Iraq. Upon graduation, Salih Muslim worked as an engineer in Saudi Arabia, only returning to Syria in the 1990s. In 1998, he joined the well-established Kurdish Democratic Party of Syria, but he quit in 2003 owing to what he saw as its lack of success. He then joined the newly-created PYD or Democratic Union Party that had been created in 2003—largely from the remnants of the PKK that Hafez Assad had expelled from Syria in October 1998—and became a member of its executive council.

Dr Fuad Omar (born in Damascus in 1962), was, however, chosen as the new party's first leader at its second conference and served in this role until 2010. Although Fuad Omar claimed to accept the militant philosophy of Abdullah Ocalan's PKK, he also incongruously maintained that 'we do not believe in violence and solving issues through military means'.[5] Nevertheless, by 2008, Fuad Omar had been sentenced to prison and was living in exile in Belgium.

Thus, Salih Muslim only became the *serok* (president) of the PYD in 2010, despite being in prison for two or three months every year since 2003. However, he was soon forced to flee from his Syrian home to the Qandil mountains in Iraqi Kurdistan where he lived in a camp maintained by the PYD and PKK. For whatever reasons, the Assad regime allowed him to return to Syria in April 2011 just after the civil war broke out. He quickly became the surprisingly successful leader of the rejuvenated PYD. On 16 June 2012, he was re-elected as the PYD's co-chair at its extraordinary fifth party congress, while a woman, Asia Abdullah, was chosen as the other co-chair. It is clear, however, that Salih Muslim remained the party's primary leader.

Salih Muslim currently plays a complicated, but potentially important role in the Syrian uprising against Bashar Assad that has been raging since March 2011. Some argue that in effect Salih Muslim's PYD has become *Shabiha* (thuggish militiamen of Assad), unlike the other twelve to fifteen or so Kurdish groups in Syria.[6] Indeed, as mentioned above, Assad's late father Hafez Assad (died 2000) long granted the PKK a virtual alliance and safe house in Syria until Turkey's threat to go to war in 1998 forced him to sign the Adana Agreement under which Syria finally expelled the PKK.

However, once Turkey began supporting the Syrian Arab Spring uprising against Assad in 2011, the Syrian regime apparently began playing the PKK card again against Turkey by inviting Salih Muslim back and allowing him to operate relatively freely.[7] Assad had already sought to appease the Syrian Kurds—who at maybe 2.2 million constitute the largest ethnic minority in Syria—by lifting long-running restrictions against them. In this newly found role Salih Muslim has strongly opposed Turkish influence upon the opposition SNC, its successor the National Coalition of Syrian Revolutionary and Opposition Forces and the Kurdish National Council (KNC), regarding them as lackeys of Turkey and other outside forces.[8] Indeed, he once went so far as to state that Turkey, the supporter of the SNC, was a greater enemy than Assad.[9]

As a result, the PYD was the only Syrian Kurdish party that boycotted the eleven-party KNC opposition conference held in the KRG capital of Irbil in January 2012 under the auspices of the KRG president Massoud Barzani. As already noted, Barzani has been working closely with Turkey in recent years to improve the economic and political position of the KRG and also, at the behest of Turkey, pressuring the PKK to come to a settlement with Turkey. Thus the PKK, as the enemy of Turkey, has not been on good terms with Barzani. This is all the more so given Salih Muslim's position that Barzani supports the KNC, which is supported by Turkey to the detriment of the true interests of the Syrian Kurds. Accordingly, Salih Muslim declared, 'We see that this effort by the Kurdistan President [Barzani] for reconciliation in Syria will lead to the disintegration of [the] Syrian Kurds.'[10] These strained ties between the PYD and Barzani's KRG are not likely to improve in the near future.

The following month (February 2012), Salih Muslim also declined to attend the SNC's Friends of Syria conference held in Tunisia, which brought together representative of some sixty states and numerous Syrian opposition groups. Thus, Salih Muslim's actions have served to further fracture Kurdish unity in Syria and oppose Turkish aid to the Syrian opposition, actions that have helped Assad continue to survive. Salih

Muslim's dealings have also made it more difficult for the United States and other Western states to effectively support the Syrian opposition. However, Salih Muslim denies any support for Assad and can point to members of his PYD being detained by the Syrian regime and his own denunciations of the regime.[11] Thus, the alliance between Salih Muslim's PYD and Assad is more implicit and only partial.

With its military wing the Yekineyen Parastina Gel (YPG)[12] or Peoples Defence Units, the PYD has become the largest, best-armed and most-disciplined Syrian Kurdish party. Salih Muslim's weakness, however, might be the traditional PKK inclination his PYD has inherited: to either be the unchallenged leader of the Kurds, therefore reluctant to join in any alliance of equals, or go it alone. Indeed the so-called Supreme Kurdish Council Barzani had tenuously patched together between the PYD and the KNC in July 2012 seemed to be unravelling by October 2012. Furthermore, at the end of October 2012 thirty people were reported killed in Aleppo as a result of fighting between the PYD and the Free Syrian Army (FSA), the supposed military arm of the SNC.[13]

This supposed Kurdish fighting against the FSA—with a few exceptions—was really against Salafists[14] or jihadists who were Sunni Muslim extremists waging violent struggle to achieve an ideal Islamic society and were only loosely connected to the FSA, which itself was becoming more a mere loosely coordinated umbrella collection of different, even hostile, groups. Increasingly, one was now hearing more about individual militias and brigades as being Assad's opposition, instead of the military FSA and political SNC. Even so, however, to a large extent the PYD saw the FSA as Turkey's hireling army, while the FSA viewed the PYD as a proxy for the Assad regime. The creation of the National Coalition of Syrian Revolutionary and Opposition Forces in November 2012 to replace the moribund SNC did not solve these difficulties. Even more, however, conflict among the Syrian Kurds themselves threatened, given the divisions between the PYD and KNC.[15]

Intra-Kurdish fighting

Even before the Syrian civil war and current intra-Kurdish infighting, the Syrian Kurdish Democratic Concord Party (SKDCP) or Wifaq had split from the PYD in 2004. This schism soon led to violence. Kamal Shahin, the new party's founder and a former PYD leader, was murdered by PKK militants on 17 February 2005, and Kamuran Muhammad in August 2005. Nadeem Yusif managed to escape a similar fate in September 2005. Kamal Shahin's assassins were apprehended and sentenced in Sulaymaniya in Iraqi Kurdistan. The PYD accused Wifaq members of collaborating with Damascus against them.[16] Rekeftin (Reconciliation), led by Fawzi Shingali, represented another small party that split from the PYD in 2004. It still exists, but plays only a very marginal role.

Further intra-Kurdish fighting involving the PYD occurred in March and April 2013. The PYD claimed the right to hold a monopoly on the use of force and wanted no rival militias allowed. However, the Jabhat al-Akrad (a Kurdish unit headed by Haji Ahmed Kurdi in the FSA), the Salah al-Din Brigade (mainly from Afrin) and the Mishaal Tammo Battalion (consisting of army defectors) were small, additional Kurdish militias loosely associated with the FSA and also battling the Salafists.[17] The KDP of Massoud Barzani accused the PYD of being involved in killings, arrests and kidnappings of members of other Kurdish parties.[18] On 18 May 2013 the PYD's *Asayesh* (security forces) arrested seventy-four members of the Democratic Party of Syria, who had undergone training in the KRG by the KDP. Then at the end of June the PYD killed at least six other Kurds and injured many more in the city of Amuda just west of Qamishli. The PYD also detained dozens more and burned down youth and cultural centres of the rival Kurdish Yekiti and Azadi parties.

Kurdish opponents of the PYD chanted, 'He who kills his people is a traitor.' The opposing Kurdish KNC charged that the PYD was trying to impose its authority on Kurds who did not want to accept it and even accused the PYD of working with the Assad regime by protecting landing sites in nearby Kobani used by the regime's helicopters. Even the US State Department condemned the PYD's actions. Less than two weeks later, a group of Kurdish intellectuals held another anti-PYD protest in Qamishli; the PYD responded with sticks and knives.[19] In August 2013, Siamend Hajo, an employee of the independent KurdWatch in Berlin, who had been closely covering the PYD, was threatened with death for his criticism of its human rights abuses.[20]

Despite these problems, Salih Muslim responded via e-mail to this author that 'I would like to state that the Kurdish Forces (YPG and Asayish) are in [a] self defence position [and] they never attacked the others'.[21] In a wide-ranging interview he held earlier in November 2011,[22] Salih Muslim blamed Turkey for spreading rumours that he was behind several recent assassinations of various other Kurdish leaders in Syria such as Mishaal Tammo who, as analysed above, was assassinated in October 2011, as well as more recently Abdullah Bedro's three sons, Muhammed Xelef Ciwan, Nesredin Berhik and Dr. Serzad Hac Resid.[23]

Salih Muslim, however, readily admitted that 'we apply Apo's [the imprisoned PKK leader Abdullah Ocalan] philosophy and ideology to Syria.' The PYD leader continued by declaring that, 'we have put forth a project: "democratic autonomy".' This term, of course, comes right out of Ocalan's latest books published in English.[24] Salih Muslim elaborated that 'we as the Kurdish Freedom Movement [...] reject classical models like federalism, con-federalism, self-government, and autonomy', explaining that 'our goal is the formation of a new Kurdish society, the formation of a free person, a person with free will [...] The point is to renew society from the bottom up.'[25]

Salih Muslim also demanded, 'the constitutional recognition of the Kurds as a second ethnicity in Syria.' Although this demand might make Assad think twice about his tactical ally, Salih Muslim further claimed that, 'the PYD has opened Kurdish cultural centre and language schools [...] We are profiting from the unrest.' However, he also criticised the opposition SNC for signing an agreement with Turkey, 'We consider anyone who does not publicly take a stand against the Turkish position to be one of Turkey's henchmen.'[26] In a later text conversation,[27] Salih Muslim cited the cryptic proverb 'a wise enemy is better than an ignorant friend' to explain how the Assad regime viewed him and why the PYD sometimes seemed to be co-operating with the Syrian regime.

To explain the PYD's new-found strength, Azad Muhiyuddin, a member of the Movement of the Youth in the West (apparently an allusion to the Kurds living in Syria constituting western Kurdistan) said, 'they [the PYD] have taken on the conflicts that the [other Kurdish] parties [in Syria] have been waging for more than forty years [...] The PYD is trying to show the people that it represents the interests of the Kurds [...] They offer numerous services and are active in social welfare [...] Thus the people are joining those who do things for them.'[28] Even more important to explain the relative strength of the PYD, of course, is that it is armed while the KNC is still largely not.

Although it is difficult to see clearly through the complexity that is Syria today, Salih Muslim's PYD is likely to continue to grow in strength within the multifaceted Kurdish movement in Syria because the other

Kurdish parties are so divided and therefore weak. In addition, Salih Muslim has the proven organisational skills of the PKK to support him as well as his own abilities. If Turkey were to intervene in Syria, it would face the possibility of Salih Muslim helping to lead vigorous Kurdish opposition as part of those Syrian nationalists who inevitably would oppose such outside interference. The same would apply to any intervention from Barzani's KRG. Finally, Salih Muslim also has positioned himself in the morass of Syrian politics so as to have connections with both the Assad regime and its opposition. Thus, if either side ultimately wins in Syria, Salih Muslim's PYD is likely to still be standing.

De facto Syrian Kurdish autonomy

Although the immediate active momentum from the Qamishli (*Serhildan*) uprising in March 2004 soon petered out, newly formed youth groups independent from the traditional political parties as well as local coordination committees continued the spirit of discontent. These included the Kurdish Youth Movement, the Union of Kurdish Youth Coordination, the Kurdish Youth Union and the Avahi Union. These youth committees established a non-hierarchical, democratic administrative structure that proved viable.

During its third party congress in 2007, the PYD established a Central Coordinating Committee (CCC) as a governing body with eleven members (increased to twenty-four in August 2012 during the fourth party congress) and with political, youth, cultural and women's departments, among others. The CCC also coordinated the work of Peoples Local Committees or local governance bodies. Equally important, the PYD also established its own militia, the YPG already mentioned above. Thus, even before the civil war broke out in March 2011, the PYD had begun to project an image as concerned and able compared with other Kurdish parties.

Then on 19 July 2012, as previously noted, the Assad regime suddenly pulled most of its troops and authority out of the Kurdish regions of north-eastern Syria, which lie just below Turkey's southern border, to concentrate on holding its position in the heartland of the country.[29] Kobani (Ayn al-Arab) proved to be the first city occupied by the PYD, followed in short order by Amuda and Afrin the following day. On 21 July, YPG forces took Derik (al-Malikyah) and a day later Serekaniye

(Ras al-Ayn) and Dirbesi (al-Darbasiyah). By the beginning of August 2012, PYD forces occupied most Kurdish cities with the exception of Qamishli and Hasaka, which, however, also had considerable numbers of Arabs, among other groups residing there. The speed with which all this occurred led to speculation that there was an agreement between the regime and the PYD. Indeed, on 7 April 2011, Decree 49 had already granted long-sought-for citizenship to the *ajanib*.

In the event, the largely Kurdish province of Hasaka for a time remained mostly free of the fighting that was raging in the west of Syria, which however did involve Kurdish areas in Kurd Dagh (Afrin) as well as Aleppo. While these struggles occurred, as already noted, less was attributed to the loosely organised umbrella FSA military and its disjointed political associate the SNC and more began to be heard in the name of individual militias and brigades.

This situation, of course, allowed the emerging PYD governmental structures greater room to grow. De facto PYD autonomy continued to develop after the civil war had begun when, on 12 December 2011, the PYD created the Peoples Council of Western Kurdistan (PCWK) as an elected local assembly of 320 members with executive and legislative branches to provide social services and a modicum of authority in places undergoing anarchy and violence due to the civil war. The PCWK has local representatives such as mayors throughout Syrian Kurdistan including the Kurdish quarter in Aleppo, to carry out the work of municipalities instead of the Assad regime. In addition, the PYD confusingly formed local, self-organised civilian structures under the label of the Tevgera Civaka Demokratik (TEV-DEM) or the Movement for a Democratic Society and also known as the Democratic Popular Movement. Also still operating in September 2013, the Supreme Kurdish Council was yet another entity that supposedly sought to achieve administrative coordination between the PYD and the other Kurdish parties. All this seemingly overlapping and bewildering proliferation of institutional forms, however, gave the PYD an enormous edge over the other political parties in organisational strength and effectiveness. In addition, these various bodies the PYD has created in Syria, supposedly to begin implementing grass-roots democracy, only pretend to include the local population; in practice they decide little. The PKK leadership in the Qandil mountains and Abdullah Ocalan in Imrali are the ones who really rule through various PKK/PYD commanders responsible for different areas. As of

September 2013, Shahin Cello from Kobani is reportedly the com-mander-in-chief of all military units of the PYD/YPG in Syria. For-merly, he was a member of the PKK central committee and a leading PKK operative in Europe.[30] Nevertheless, this proliferation of govern-mental institutions led to comparisons with how the KRG had been ini-tially created back in 1991. Initially strongest in Afrin (Kurd Dagh) in the west, the PYD also now began to show strength in the far eastern province of Hasaka or Jazira.

The resulting Syrian Kurdish autonomy caused great apprehension in Turkey because suddenly PKK flags were flying just across its southern border with Syria; what had been just 500 miles of border, with Iraqi Kurdistan (the KRG) only, had overnight metastasised into 750 miles. A second or even a pan-Kurdish state seemed possible. Ankara feared that this newly won Kurdish Syrian position would serve as an unwanted model for Turkey's own disaffected Kurds and the PKK. Turkey also feared that the Syrian Kurdish autonomous area bordering the KRG might seek to unite with the KRG and form for Turkey the nightmare of a pan-Kurd-ish state. Thus, Turkey hoped that its influence over the Syrian opposi-tion and the KRG would help to control pan-Kurdish ambitions.

The earliest incidents of Kurdish-FSA (actually Salafists or Sunni Muslim extremists) fighting actually had already occurred at the end of June and the beginning of July 2012 in the city of Afrin in the north-western area of the country known as Kurd Dagh. By October 2012, fighting between the two sides was continuing in the west and also began in Serekaniye. Confusingly, regime air strikes also took place here at the same time. In addition, PYD clashes occurred against other Kurdish groups, particularly the Yekiti party. However, at this point, the analysis will turn to the Salafist Jabhat al-Nusra group and its struggle against the regime, which, however, given the focus of this study, most impor-tantly also involved the Kurds.

Jabhat al-Nusra

Jabhat al-Nusra (the Victory or Liberation Front) in general grew out of the jihadist/Salafist radical Islamic movements spawned by al-Qaeda, and specifically out of Abu Musab al-Zarqawi's Al-Qaeda in Iraq (AQI) force that fought the United States in Iraq during its horrific civil war following the overthrow of Saddam Hussein. Ironically, the Assad regime had helped to sponsor AQI as a way to confront the United States, so when its immediate successors turned on Assad in his hour of need it was a classic case of blowback. (The US support for jihadist groups in Afghanistan during the 1980s also led to blowback against the United States on the part of the Taliban and al-Qaeda after September 2001.)

Joined by Salafists from other countries in the Middle East (especially Saudi Arabia, Libya, Tunisia, Egypt, Jordan, Lebanon and Iraq, among others), Europe (Britain, France and Belgium, among others), and even—in smaller numbers—the Caucasus (Chechnya), south Asia and North America, these radicals crossed the porous borders of Syria through border gates from Turkey (Tel Abyad/Gire Spi) and Iraq (Tel Kochar) to announce al-Nusra's creation on 23 January 2012. Its leader, Abu Mohammad al-Golani, swore allegiance to al-Qaeda's leader Ayman al-Zawahiri,[31] but offered only co-operation with another of the many other Salafist groups that had entered Syria, the Islamic State of Iraq and al-Sham [Syria] (ISIS), also known as the Islamic State of Iraq and the Levant (ISIL). Despite several other Salafist and secular organisations, al-Nusra quickly earned a reputation for being the most militarily effective of all the anti-Assad rebel groups. The United States, Britain, Australia and the United Nations, among others, responded by officially stamping al-Nusra as a terrorist organisation.

Al-Nusra's reputed goal was to overthrow the infidel (Alawite) Assad regime—which it viewed as *takfiri* or apostates to Islam—and create a pan-Islamic state under sharia law and a new Sunni Caliphate. These militants also saw their fellow Sunni brothers being slaughtered by the Assad regime and viewed victory in Syria as a base for eventually retaking al-Quds (Jerusalem) and the al-Aqsa Mosque. They quickly combined their battlefield prowess with providing social services that enabled them to win over some of the local population whose territory they seized.

The new organisation contained a hierarchy of religious bodies, with a small *majlis* or *shura* (council) at the top. Each region also had its own emir, commander and/or sheikh. It referred to the United States and Israel as its enemies and, in contrast to its supposed secular allies in the FSA, warned against Western intervention in Syria.

Al-Nusra was estimated to have approximately 5,000 members with a structure that varied across Syria. Most of the new organisation's fighting was against the regime; in Aleppo and Hasaka, where it also fell into conflict with the Kurds, it was organised along conventional military lines in units divided into brigades and regiments. Although al-Nusra supposedly constituted part of the FSA, in practice it largely operated independently and seemed bent on eventually hijacking what had started out as a democratic, secular revolution. Secularists, for example, accused al-Nusra of committing numerous atrocities against captured fighters and civilians, but the Salafists retorted that they did not target civilians, and actually brought medical supplies to those places they occupied. However, one FSA leader declared that, 'we are not fighting Bashar al-Assad to go from living in an autocratic to religious prison.'[32] Thus, one could easily foresee al-Nusra turning against its supposed secular allies in the FSA when the opportunity presented itself.

Fighting versus Kurds

Although historically there have been ultra-Islamic Kurdish Sufi orders, there is an old maxim that compared with a non-believer, a Kurd is a good Muslim. This is largely true because Kurds have mostly seen Muslim Arabs deny Kurdish rights. In other words, most Kurds are more nationalist and secular than religious and thus not prone to adopt Salafist positions.

As noted above, the earliest incidents of Kurdish fighting against Salafist groups such as al-Nusra actually occurred even before the regime pulled its troops out of most Kurdish cities on 19 July 2012. Thus, at the end of June and beginning of July 2012 in the city of Afrin in the northwestern area of the country known as Kurd Dagh and also in the Kurdish neighbourhood of Ashrafiyya in Aleppo, hostilities had already broken out as al-Nusra came into contact with the local, secular-minded Kurds. The latter saw the Salafists as thugs acting on behalf of neighbouring Turkey, which was seeking to quash Kurdish influence in northern Syria and allay its fears of a breakaway Kurdish state on its southern border, while the former viewed the Kurds as de facto allies of the despised Assad regime and *takfiri*. By October 2012, fierce fighting between the two sides was also occurring in the west where it began in Serekaniye, Syria's northernmost city[33] and continued until a tenuous ceasefire occurred in February 2013. Clashes also took place in Tel Abyad (Gire Spi), Qamishli and Tel Tamr, also near the Turkish border, as well as in the city of Hasaka.

In areas under their control, al-Nusra and other Salafists hastened to impose their reactionary vision of Islam, including enforced fasting, threatening women to make them wear the hijab, kidnapping civilians and enforcing sharia (Islamic law) without considering the local diversity and cultures of the Kurds with whom they were interacting. Indeed the Salafists had particular difficulties with women, seeking to isolate them socially and politically. The Egyptian Salafist Abu Islam even issued fatwas justifying raping women in Tahrir Square as a punishment for their unveiling themselves. These religious fanatics 'consider women to be sex objects that are a permanent threat to society'.[34] Salafists also pillaged and looted Kurdish towns and villages torturing, raping and killing.

Events quickened on 16 July 2013 when al-Nusra attacked PYD female fighters in Serekaniye. Fierce fighting that cost mostly Salafist lives drove al-Nusra out of the city bordering Turkey. Most observers saw this as a major victory for the PYD and it was. However, for al-Nusra the Kurdish fighting was simply a lesser battle within the larger one against the regime taking place in the west around Aleppo. In addition, Salafist militants occupied the provincial capital of Raqqah to the south and battled to the east of Qamishli where al-Nusra seized many of Syria's oil wells that were of great importance.

If al-Nusra were to prevail, it might be in a position to establish a self-sustaining autonomous al-Qaeda statelet, which would surely represent blowback onto Turkey and thus might cause it to reconsider its immediate position regarding whom to support and oppose in Syria. However, to the west around the Kurdish city of Afrin, the Salafists and Turkey continued to impose a suffocating blockade against the Kurds. Similarly, Barzani's KDP in the far east also continued to keep the border closed with Hasaka province where the Kurds lived. On 30 July 2013 Isa Hisso, a prominent member of the PYD, was assassinated in Qashimli. Some suspected the Salafists, but others blamed the regime.

By mid-August 2013 the YPG was battling Salafists on five separate fronts in the provinces of Raqqah, Aleppo and Hasaka. Given all these pressures, the PYD called upon the international community for support against their Salafist attackers. Turkey and the PYD then did the unthinkable.

Salih Muslim negotiates with Turkey

On 25 July 2013, amid reports that the PYD was about to declare Kurdish autonomy in Syria, Turkey publicly invited Salih Muslim to Istanbul for talks. Indeed, one report claimed that the PYD had already produced a constitution for the Syrian Kurdish regions. Under its provisions, Syria would become a democratic parliamentary federal system. Western Kurdistan, with Qamishli as its capital, would be one of the federal or autonomous self-ruling regions making its own internal decisions. Kurdish and Arabic would be its official languages and self-ruling units would protect the Syrian borders from foreign intervention. This Kurdish government would be headed by a man or a woman with twenty-one ministers appointed by the parliament. Among these ministries would be: Finance, Judiciary, Tourism and Environment, Human Rights, Culture, Electricity and Defence, among others. However, Salih Muslim quickly pulled back from this constitutional proclamation, claiming that it was premature and that other viewpoints still had to be consulted.[35]

The PYD leader hastened to assure Turkey that his party's call for a local administration for Syria's Kurdish regions did not mean that it was seeking independence that would threaten Turkey, 'Our thought is to establish a provisional council of 40 to 50—maybe a hundred people.' He added that, 'this council will comprise Kurds, Syriacs, Arabs and Turkmens', and was simply a necessary ad hoc device to help alleviate the war-torn situation until the end of the civil war allowed more permanent arrangements. 'Kurds will need to have a status in the new order in Syria. But what's in question now is a provisional arrangement […] It's not about making a constitution.'[36] In addition, these PYD proposals for quasi-autonomy would help the PYD regain some of the support and popularity they had squandered by falling into intra-Kurdish fighting in Amuda and other places, as discussed above.

Although Salih Muslim had previously held secret meetings with Turkish officials, this highly visible, publicly touted encounter represented a potential U-turn or even game changer in Turkish-PYD relations. Ahmet Davutoglu, the Turkish foreign minister, explained that his country's new approach was in line with its decision to talk with the PKK leader Abdullah Ocalan about ending his organisation's three-decade insurgency.[37] Another Turkish official added, 'We have no problem with their [the PYD] aspirations […] What we do not want from any group is that they use this situation opportunistically to impose their will by force.'[38] Ismail Arslan, the pro-Kurdish Baris ve Demokrasi Partisi (BDP) or Peace and Democracy Party mayor of Ceylanpinar, Serekaniye's twin city just across the border in Turkey elaborated that Turkey 'has seen that treating the Kurds like an enemy and supporting groups like Nusra is not good for Turkey.'

Upon its conclusion, Salih Muslim claimed that his meeting had been positive and that he had conversed about security in the border regions with his Turkish interlocutors. He went on to list the following specific points that had been discussed: 1.) opening borders and border security; 2.) humanitarian aid; 3.) explaining the PYD project for interim government; and 4.) demonstrating that the PYD proposals were not a threat to Turkey. Two weeks later Salih Muslim again journeyed to Turkey for a second round of talks.

It was clear that Ankara was bent on some type of understanding, but uncertain how far this new relationship would proceed. Would Turkey actually pursue a new relationship with the Syrian Kurds as it had with those in Iraq and the PKK? Would Turkey cease its implicit support for al-Nusra before the increasingly entangled Syrian Kurdish conundrum slipped out of its grasp and hopes for a successful secular opposition to the Assad regime proved impossible to achieve? Continuing to support anti-democratic and Salafist extremists in order to suppress Syrian Kurdish desires for autonomy would seem to be a losing strategy both at home and abroad for Turkey. The many other elements of Syria's civil war, not the least of which was Assad's final standing, further complicated the equation. Squaring the proverbial circle might prove easier than implementing a successful choice among all these perceived evils.

However, these Turkish fears about the Kurds in Syria might be overblown because the Syrian Kurds remained relatively weak and divided, the mere temporary beneficiary of the Syrian civil war. As soon as that struggle was settled, the winners would likely seek to reincorporate their wayward Kurdish provinces. Moreover, if this were slow to occur, Barzani's KRG stood in a de facto alliance with Turkey and could be counted on to dampen excessive Syrian Kurdish ambitions, especially those of the PYD.

In addition, violence between the PYD and KNC among the Syrian Kurds themselves and between the PYD and the Arab-led FSA also threatened and indeed had already broken out. On the other hand, Barzani's KRG remained a two-edged sword because the Syrian Kurds might opt to join the KRG if things did not work out for their autonomous ambitions in Syria. Indeed, Barzani had already threatened to intervene in Syria to help his Kurdish brethren against their Salafist foes.[39] Clearly the Syrian Kurds were in a state of flux, especially as long as the civil war continued. Thus, the final chapter will consider what the future might hold.

10

THE FUTURE

It is unlikely that the Kurds in Syria will return to the abyss of the forgotten. On the other hand, their future remains murky and will largely be determined by the results of the Syrian civil war. If one side or the other wins a decisive victory, it will seek to reduce the Kurds to a lower status than they presently enjoy. However, given the Kurdish empowerment that stemmed from the civil war, it would be impossible to put the Kurdish genie completely back into the bottle of the forgotten from whence it has sprung. Thus, if Syria is reunited by the Assad regime or its opposition, there will be no return to the days of the *ajanib*. Decree 49 issued on 7 April 2011 paved the way for these stateless people to finally become Syrian citizens.[1] (*Maktoumeen*, however, were not included.) The Kurds will continue to enjoy at least some of their newly won political, social and cultural rights.

From the present perspective of September 2013, however, what seems more likely is that a united Syria will not be able to be put back together again. If so, there are a number of alternative futures for the Kurds. If Turkey arrives at a satisfactory definitive settlement with the PKK, the Syrian Kurds might seek to become associated in some manner with Turkey. After all the PYD of Salih Muslim is closely associated with the PKK and is by far the strongest Syrian Kurdish party, as has been shown in previous chapters. If its elder brother the PKK and the elder statesman Abdullah Ocalan accept Turkey, the PYD and Salih Muslim might see fit to follow in their footsteps instead of risking life in a broken Syria. Turkey not only continues to become more democratic and thus acceptable to Kurdish nationalists, but also offers the Kurds in Syria the six-teenth largest state economy in the world. No matter what they do, the landlocked Kurds in Syria would obviously require good relations with Turkey to enjoy any chance of economic success.

Further, if Turkey joined the EU, as it has been formally seeking to do since 2005, the Syrian Kurds would suddenly become part of this most advanced economic bloc that also offers considerable political protection to its members. The PKK model analysed in a previous chapter would have led ironically to a successful moderate future. Interestingly, Turkish EU membership would also offer the KRG in northern Iraq close ties with the EU given the de facto alliance between Turkey and the KRG. Even more, of course, the Kurds in Turkey would also enter the EU by definition. A strong and democratic Turkey might offer the vast major-ity of the Kurds in the world an incredibly bright future. For their part, the Kurds ironically would offer Turkey the Kemalist security it has always sought to the detriment of the Kurds, but now with the support and co-operation of the Kurds because it would now be to the benefit of the Kurds. What just a decade ago might have seemed counterfactual would have become reality.

The KRG model would be another possibility if Syria cannot be recon-stituted. Within this future, the Kurds in Syria would join an already suc-cessfully functioning Kurdish state, the only one in modern times. Given the longtime prestige of Mulla Mustafa Barzani (1903–79) and now his son Massoud Barzani, the president of the KRG, as well as that of Jalal Talabani, the other main Iraqi Kurdish leader and much admired presi-dent of Iraq, becoming part of the KRG would probably appeal to many Kurds in Syria (with the exception of the PYD), especially given the KRG's political and economic achievements in recent years. Important too to remember is that the present borders that politically divide the Kurds between Syria, Turkey and Iraq are seen (and rightfully so) as arti-ficial and lacking in legitimacy. It would not prove so difficult for the Kurds in Syria to unite with the KRG. For this to occur, however, both Turkey and the PYD would have to approve, a stretch of any imagina-tion. Still, stranger futures have emerged.

The third future for the Kurds in a postwar Syria would be some type of federal or semi-autonomous existence. Sherkoh Abbas, the president of the Kurdistan National Assembly of Syria (KNAS), advocates such a federal future for his countrymen, and no doubt others do too.[2] However, the KNAS is simply a small exile group. More realistic and important would be to analyse the future envisioned by the PYD.

Democratic autonomy

The Kurds in Syria have enjoyed de facto autonomy since the regime suddenly pulled its troops out of most of the Kurdish areas on 19 July 2012. The previous chapter described the supposedly temporary institutions created to implement this autonomy at some length. As also mentioned in the previous chapter, Salih Muslim explained at the time that 'we apply Apo's [the imprisoned PKK leader Abdullah Ocalan] philosophy and ideology to Syria'.[3]

Surveying the situation, the umbrella Koma Civaken Kurdistan (KCK) or Kurdistan Communities Union that included both the PKK and PYD, among others, proudly declared that, 'Ocalan's Democratic Modernity perspective […] which is based on gender equality and aims to bring the society to power, not the state or the government, has been successfully put into practice in Rojava.'[4] Candidly, the KCK admitted that the PYD's Peoples Defence Units or YPG were the main reason that the Kurdish autonomy had been able to survive, but also argued that, 'the democratic society reality at the same time constitutes a strong defence power'. This situation was defined as, 'where all circles of the society, from children to elders, and all ethnic and belief groups do freely get organised' and 'leave no room for the survival of statist anti-democratic powers.' Indeed, the KCK even claimed that the Kurds were 'paving the way for Syria's democratisation and liberation' and 'setting an example for the achievement of democratisation in the Middle East region.'

The PYD was proposing a type of bottom-up form of civic organisation of everyone including non-Kurds that would supposedly bypass traditional governmental types and act as if the Kurds' division into non-contiguous population centres did not matter. In an e-mail to the author, for example, Salih Muslim claimed that, 'we think the separation of the areas wouldn't be [a] problem because […] no borders will be drawn around the Kurds so they can get their rights wherever they are.'[5] The PYD leader seemed oblivious to the fact that historically the Kurds' separation was one of the main reasons they were so much weaker and almost forgotten compared with the Kurds in Turkey, Iraq and even Iran. Only the chaos and breakdown of the regime's control had allowed the

Kurds in Syria so much autonomy and hopes for the future. It is also necessary to remember that most of the other Kurdish parties in Syria loosely organised as the Kurdish National Council did not concur with the PYD's proposed future. On the other hand, given the PYD's preponderance of power among the Kurds, this disagreement from the other parties was probably not as important as it might seem at first.

Murray Bookchin

Before dismissing the PYD's claims as merely utopian and too vague to be practical, it would be useful to analyse exactly what the PYD was proposing: a vision of a decentralised and democratised Middle East based on various radical intellectual theories, the most important of which were those propounded by Murray Bookchin (1921–2006), an otherwise obscure American libertarian socialist author, orator, philosopher and pioneer in the ecology movement as well as various feminists, leftist Foucauldians and critical Marxists.

Born in New York to Russian Jewish immigrants, Murray Bookchin took part in the Communist Party youth movement, but broke with Stalinism in the late 1930s. He then joined the Trotskyites, but left them in the 1950s because of their hierarchical organisation. From this point he considered himself a libertarian socialist and taught at several different schools. He also founded the social ecology movement based on anarchist, libertarian socialist and ecological thought. Bookchin believed that earlier attempts to create a utopia had failed because of the necessity of toil and drudgery. However, modern technology had eliminated the need for these kinds of debilitating work.

Our Synthetic Environment, his first of many books, was published a few months before Rachel Carson's groundbreaking *Silent Spring* in 1962. Bookchin's book described a broad range of environmental problems, but earned him little recognition because of his political radicalism. Later in life he decided that anarchism in the United States was too individualistic and publicly broke with it in 1999. He then proceeded to propound his ideas with a new political ideology he called Communalism, a type of libertarian socialism that retained his ideas about assembly democracy and the necessity of decentralisation of settlement, power, money, influence, agriculture and manufacturing, among others.

In his work so admired by Abdullah Ocalan[6] Bookchin postulated two ideals of political organisation: the Hellenic and the Roman. The first stood for a participatory-democratic form to which Bookchin claimed allegiance, while the second represented a centralist and statist type, which he rejected.[7] The Roman model became the dominant one in modern society, while the Hellenic one existed briefly in the form of the Paris Commune of 1871, the soviets in Russia during the early days of the revolution in 1917 and the Spanish revolution in 1936. The Roman model commanded a herd of subjects, while the Hellenic one boasted an active citizenship.[8]

Bookchin defined confederalism as 'the interlinking of communities with one another through recallable deputies mandated by municipal citizen's assemblies [which were] alternative to the nation-state.'[9] In another work, Bookchin wrote that confederalism was 'a network of administrative councils whose members are elected from popular face-to-face democratic alliances, in the various villages, towns, and even neighborhoods of large cities.'[10] As Lenin claimed in his early days, these bodies did not make policy, but simply administrated things. Power supposedly remained in the hands of the people themselves. As Bookchin explained, 'The members of these councils are strictly mandated, recallable, and responsible to the assemblies that choose them for the purpose of coordinating and administering the policies formulated by the assemblies themselves.'[11] He further noted that, 'their function is thus a purely administrative and practical one, not a policy making one like the function of representatives in republican systems of government.' Therefore, there was no rationalist fiction of a 'social contract' in which the people had reputedly consented to be ruled by the few in the name of the people. Bookchin would argue that this concept of the social contract simply operated as a justification for the capitalist rationale for power.

Bookchin further theorised that democratic confederalism (democratic autonomy) would mature 'when placing local farms, factories, and other enterprises in local municipal hands' occurred or 'when a community […] begins to manage its own economic resources in an interlinked way with other communities.'[12] The economy would be run by confederal councils and thus would be 'neither collectivized nor privatized […] [but] common.'[13] Bookchin's 'radically new configuration of society',[14] that has so strongly influenced Abdullah Ocalan and supposedly Salih Muslim, may be considered a type of alternative politics for going beyond the traditional state.

Thus, the following analysis will seek to analyse what has been termed variously democratic autonomy, democratic confederalism or radical democracy, among other terms—that is, the societal organisation that would serve as an alternative to the traditional nation-state and its economic structures and which Abdullah Ocalan, the role model for the PYD, sees as an ideal for the future of the Kurds and various other groups in the Middle East. In so doing this author owes much to the earlier analysis and interpretations of Joost Jongerden and Ahmet Hamdi Akkaya.[15]

Further analysis

To begin with, let us recall the mention in the previous chapter of the peoples' councils that were established in the Kurdish regions and through which the Kurds began to take greater responsibility for, and control of, their daily lives as well as the places where they were living. By referring to these councils in the context of democratic autonomy, the Kurds were indicating that they were not just thinking in terms of local initiatives, but also envisioning a larger political project. Given the seemingly inherent violence associated with the traditional state, democratic autonomy was going to be a new way of doing politics peacefully.

Basic to the traditional concept of the state is Max Weber's classic definition as the entity that holds a monopoly on the use of legitimate violence. Unfortunately, the modern state's systematic use of violence to maintain itself has served to undermine the very legitimacy it claims to possess through its supposed right to employ violence. This situation has been tormenting the Kurds in particular, for when the state uses violence against them it is deemed legitimate, but when the Kurds respond likewise it is called terrorism. Indeed the mere expression of Kurdish identity is often regarded as an existential threat to the state in which they live. In an ironic inversion of von Clausewitz, politics has become the continuation of war.

Given the seemingly inherent violence associated with the traditional state, democratic autonomy is envisaged as being a new way of doing politics, a way in which to think of government beyond the state. In one of his seminal articles, Murray Bookchin wrote that, 'perhaps the greatest single failing of movements for social reconstruction is their lack of a politics that will carry people beyond the limits established by the status quo.'[16] Thus, it was imperative to reach beyond the focus of traditional statecraft and market.[17] Similarly, from prison, Abdullah Ocalan has written that, 'the defining feature of democratic nation solution [democratic autonomy] is that it seeks a solution outside the state.'[18] This leads to the more direct, less representative autonomous capacities of the people in which they produce the necessary desired conditions for living through direct engagement and collaboration with each other. In autonomist Marxist literature, this concept is referred to as self-valorisation. Democratic confederalism or autonomy can be viewed as a bottom-up system of government.

One local leader of the pro-Kurdish BDP in Turkey saw this novel project as an alternative both to capitalism, which historically found its ideological, organisational and political expression in the state, and 'real existing socialism' or communism, which failed to develop political alternatives and thus has collapsed. This local BDP leader elaborated that democratic autonomy did not seek to take over state power, but to develop alternative forms of power through self-organisation. Like the soviets or local governmental forms in Russia before 1917, local councils had already existed covertly in the Kurdish areas of Syria since 2007.

When the PYD took power on 19 July 2012, these entities suddenly popped up openly all over, organising justice and mediating conflicts among the people. They also assumed the responsibility for organising social life and providing for basic social services while the civil war was raging. To prevent speculation and bribery, an administrative committee was established for the sale of bread. In Derik, the local council was involved in the equal distribution of gasoline. In addition, the local councils also provided for the first school teaching the Kurdish language. Hundreds of students, for example, enrolled in the Martyr Osman School in Kobani within just a few months. Other schools soon followed in various cities. Self defence units (the YPG) were also established. They were able to oust the regime's forces and keep the oppositionist FSA at bay. As noted in the previous chapter, the PCWK was created on 12 December 2011 as an umbrella under which the local councils could be organised. As Salih Muslim concluded, 'We don't need the central authorities or the main government. Everywhere […] we have a kind of self-rule, self-government, and till now it is very successful.'[19]

Since 2005, the PKK and all its affiliated organisations including the PYD have supposedly been restructured according to this ideal of democratic autonomy in an umbrella entity called the Koma Civaken Kurdistan (KCK) or Kurdistan Communities Union. According to Abdullah Ocalan, the KCK is organised in the form of assemblies from the bottom up as an alternative to the traditional nation-state: 'It is the umbrella organization [...] composed of economic and ecological communities, democratic compatriots, and open cultural identities.'[20]

Elaborating, the PKK leader added that 'the KCK can be defined as the democratisation of civil society [...] as the umbrella organisation of civil society' (p. 94). In addition, 'the KCK model is not the opposite of a union of states but a democratic confederalism; it is a parallel and complementary union of civil society, created because of pressing social needs' (p. 98). Economically, 'the KCK will be in a position to defend society and the environment against the devastating effects of capitalist modernity, with its sole aim at achieving maximum profits' (p. 96). Socially, 'the KCK system [...] will have a symbiotic relationship with the state as well as a competition' (Ibid.). Regarding the security aspect, 'the KCK will have to have its own defence forces' (p. 97). Diplomatically, 'the KCK [...] proposes a system that resolves problems without differentiating between ethnicities and nations but that takes denominational, ethnic, and national differences into account' (Ibid.).

The Demokratik Toplum Kongresi (DTK) or Democratic Society Congress was established in Turkey in October 2007 as a structured assembly of local councils to implement what Ocalan has called 'democracy without the state'.[21] This edifice is supposedly organised at the village, urban neighbourhood, district, city and regional levels, but also reputedly has an intricate super-structure including a Permanent Chamber of 101 delegates, a Coordination Council of thirteen delegates including two chairs, one male and the other female, and an Executive Committee of five delegates. Since being expelled from the Turkish parliament when his party, the Demokratik Toplum Partisi (DTP) or Democratic Society Party was banned on 11 December 2009, Ahmet Turk has served as the co-chair of the DTK along with his female colleague Aysel Tugluk.

In a move that infuriated the Turkish government, the DTK declared democratic autonomy within Turkey in July 2011.[22] However, Aysel Tugluk also added that the Kurdish people would remain loyal to Turkey's national unity. Understandably, Ankara saw the DTK and KCK as an attempt to establish an alternative Kurdish government on Turkish soil and continued its wholesale arrests of members of these organisations for terrorism. Although precise figures are unavailable, Human Rights Watch has asserted that several thousand are currently on trial, and that another 605 are in pretrial detention on KCK/PKK-related terrorism charges.[23]

Final observations

Democratic autonomy seems to be a term that nobody can clearly define, although obviously it entails the general wish to implement some type of effective local government. Beyond this, the detailed attempt at further analysis above may only help contribute to this lack of clarity. Nevertheless, it is hoped that the analysis in this chapter will at least help give us some idea of what type of future the PYD, purportedly, would like to implement for the Kurds in Syria.

Several basic problems with this stated desire to achieve such a utopian future exist, however. First of all, despite all the positive sounding rhetoric, what would such a project really look like? Would the authorities have to shoot the private property owners who do not want to cede their assets to the collective, as Stalin did with the *kulaks* in the 1930s? Who would really support such a programme? In addition, as illustrated by its actions against its rivals in the Kurdish community itself, the PYD in practice has no intention of allowing local councils to make the crucial decisions. Despite its rhetoric, the PYD in action has exuded a strong will to rule and be obeyed. Those who disagree have felt the wrath of the PYD in the form of societal pressure, arrest, torture and even execution.

For their part, although the other Kurdish parties in Syria loosely organised into the Kurdish National Council have co-operated with the PYD at times, they also have demonstrated the wish to follow their own alternative paths. Thus, even if the PYD truly wanted to implement some type of bottom-up rule that stressed local governmental, citizenship control, it is not clear how many Kurds in Syria would voluntarily agree to follow such a lead.

What is more, the KRG in Iraq, the only successful example of a Kurdish government and, in effect, state in modern times, is just that, a de facto state. Thus it has no intention of committing suicide upon the nebulous concept of democratic autonomy. In practice, of course, the PKK and PYD, with their strongly centralised leadership, also represent anything but advocates for locally-based administration. Indeed, if the oft-postponed first pan-Kurdish congress in Irbil ever does convene it will be interesting to see what future for democratic autonomy, if any, will emerge. However, the real reason for the congress being postponed stems from disagreements between the KRG and PKK/PYD over how to allocate seats between them. In a similar debate to that which was once played out between the large and small states at the US Constitutional Convention in 1787, the KRG is arguing for representational equality between the various parts of Kurdistan despite their different populations, while the PKK/PYD demands greater representation in accordance with its larger population.[24]

Even more, however, the history of such anarchical ideas as propounded by Murray Bookchin and now Abdullah Ocalan, while maybe theoretically appealing to some, have proved impossible to implement in practice. The Bolshevik Revolution in Russia, for example, quickly degenerated into a totalitarian Stalinist state of terror that proved the opposite of local democracy. The reality of today's world is that people need strong governmental institutions to be effective. While Western democracy has many problems—as pointed out by the former communists of the Soviet Union and theoreticians like Murray Bookchin and Abdullah Ocalan—anarchical alternatives that seek to eliminate the state have not worked in practice. Thus, if the PYD or some other Kurdish organisation or group of organisations eventually comes to power in a post-Assad Syria, it will soon allow these vague concepts of democratic autonomy to be shelved or at best reinterpreted along more practical lines.

Indeed, as discussed in the previous chapter, the various bodies the PYD has created in Syria, supposedly to begin implementing democratic autonomy, only pretend to include the local population, but in practice decide little. In reality, the PKK leadership in the Qandil mountains and Abdullah Ocalan in Imrali are the ones who really rule through various PKK/PYD commanders responsible for different areas. As of September 2013, Shahin Cello from Kobani is reported to be the commander-in-chief of all military units of the PYD/YPG in Syria. Formerly, he was a member of the PKK central committee and a leading PKK operative in Europe.

NOTES

INTRODUCTION

1. See Tejel, Jordi, *Syria's Kurds: History, Politics and Society*, London and New York: Routledge, 2009; Montgomery (Allsopp), Harriet, *The Kurds of Syria: An Existence Denied*, Berlin: European Centre for Kurdish Studies, 2005; and Yildiz, Kerim, *The Kurds in Syria: The Forgotten People*, London: Pluto Press, 2005. More recently, see the soon to be published Allsopp, Harriet, *The Kurds of Syria: Political Parties and Identity in the Middle East*, London: I.B. Tauris, forthcoming.

2. For further background on the Kurds in Syria, see Vanly, Ismet Cheriff, 'The Kurds in Syria and Lebanon', in Kreyenbroek, Philip G. and Stefan Sperl (eds), *The Kurds: A Contemporary Overview*, London: Routledge, 1992, pp. 143–70; Nazdar, Mustafa (Ismet Cheriff Vanly), 'The Kurds in Syria', in Chaliand, Gerard (ed.), *A People Without a Country: The Kurds and Kurdistan*, New York: Olive Branch Books, 1993, pp. 194–201; Vanly, Ismet Cheriff, 'The Oppression of the Kurdish People in Syria', in Ahmed, Mohammed M. A. and Michael M. Gunter (eds), *Kurdish Exodus: From Internal Displacement to Diaspora*, Sharon, Mass.: Ahmed Foundation for Kurdish Studies, 2002, pp. 49–61; Amnesty International, *Amnesty International Report: Kurds in the Syrian Arab Republic One Year after the March 2004 Events*, 2005; and Lowe, Robert, 'Kurdish Nationalism in Syria', in Ahmed, Mohammed M. A. and Michael M. Gunter (eds), *The Evolution of Kurdish Nationalism*, Costa Mesa, CA: Mazda Publishers, 2007, pp. 287–308.

3. Cited in 'Politics & policies: pressure for change mounts in Syria', United Press International, 3 October 2005.

1. BACKGROUND

1. The leading background source in English on the Kurds in Syria is Tejel, Jordi, *Syria's Kurds: History, Politics and Society*, London and New York: Routledge, 2009. Also see Montgomery, Harriet (Allsopp), *The Kurds of Syria: An Existence Denied*, Berlin: European Centre for Kurdish Studies, 2005; and Yildiz, Kerim, *The Kurds in Syria: The Forgotten People*, London: Pluto Press, 2005. More recently, see Inter-

national Crisis Group, 'Syria's Kurds: a Struggle within a Struggle', *Middle East Report No. 136*, 22 January 2013; and Allsopp, Harriet, *The Kurds of Syria: Political Parties and Identity in the Middle East*, London: I.B. Tauris, forthcoming.

2. For background, see Khoury, Philip, *Syria and the French Mandate: The Politics of Arab Nationalism*, London: I.B. Tauris, 1987; and Fuccaro, Nelida, 'Kurds and Kurdish Nationalism in Mandatory Syria: Politics, Culture and Identity', in Vali, Abbas (ed.), *Essays on the Origins of Kurdish Nationalism*, Costa Mesa, CA: Mazda Publishers, 2003, pp. 191–217. For a useful recent analysis, see White, Benjamin, *The Emergence of Minorities in the Middle East: The Politics of Community in French Mandate Syria*, Edinburgh: Edinburgh University Press, 2011.

3. On this point, see McDowall, David, *A Modern History of the Kurds*, London and New York: I.B. Tauris, 1996, p. 4.

4. Jwaideh, Wadie, *The Kurdish National Movement: Its Origins and Development*, Syracuse: Syracuse University Press, 2006, p. 143.

5. Tejel, *Syria's Kurds*, pp. 66 and 99.

6. For more on how nations are invented rather than existing since time immemorial, see Anderson, Benedict, *Imagined Communities: Reflections on the Origin and Spread of Nationalism*, London: Verso, 1991.

7. Strohmeier, Martin, *Crucial Images in the Presentation of Kurdish National Identity: Heroes and Patriots: Traitors and Foes*, Leiden and Boston: Brill, 2003. Strohmeier also heuristically uses as guides for his analysis the work of such well-known contemporary scholars of nationalism as Anderson, Benedict, *Imagined Communities*, 1991; Connor, Walker, *Ethnonationalism: The Quest for Understanding*, Princeton: Princeton University Press, 1994; and Gellner, Ernest, *Nations and Nationalism*, Ithaca: Cornell University Press, 1983, among others.

8. *The Emergence of Kurdish Nationalism and the Sheikh Said Rebellion, 1880–1925*, Austin: University of Texas Press, 1989.

9. *Agha, Shaikh and State: The Social and Political Structure of Kurdistan*, London and New Jersey: Zed Books, 1992. In addition, of course, there are additional authors writing either in other European languages—such as Kutschera, Chris, *Le Mouvement national kurde*, Paris: Flammarion, 1979; and Behrendt, Gunter, *Nationalismus in Kurdistan: Vorgeschichte, Entstehungsbedingungen und erste Manifestationen bis 1925*, Hamburg: Dt. Orient-Inst., 1993—or Middle Eastern languages.

10. For the sake of brevity, the following page numerals refer to the Strohmeier study so that repetitive endnotes may be avoided.

11. On the other hand, one should note that the loss of their native Celtic language did not inhibit the eventual success won against England by the now English-speaking Irish nationalists.

12. Tejel, *Syria's Kurds*, p. 46.

13. Mella, Jawad, *The Colonial Policy of the Syrian Baath Party in Western Kurdistan*, London: Western Kurdistan Association, 2006.

14. On this point regarding dissimulation, 'which is related to the religious term *taqiyya*' and is a strategy of group survival used by the Shiites and other minorities to avoid repression., see Tejel, *Syria's Kurds*, p. 83.

2. THE FORGOTTEN

1. Cited in Lynch, Maureen and Perveen Ali, 'Buried Alive: Stateless Kurds in Syria', Washington: Refugees International, 2006, p. i. In addition, see Tejel, Jordi, *Syria's Kurds: History, Politics and Society*, London and New York: Routledge, 2009, pp. 51–2; and Lowe, Robert, 'Kurdish Nationalism in Syria', in Ahmed, Mohammed M. A. and Michael M. Gunter (eds), *The Evolution of Kurdish Nationalism*, Costa Mesa, CA: Mazda Publishers, 2007, pp. 294–6.

2. Cited in Lynch and Ali, 'Buried Alive', pp. 1–2.

3. On the Baath party, see Abu Jaber, Kamel S., *The Arab Ba'th Socialist Party: History, Ideology, and Organization*, Syracuse: Syracuse University Press, 1966; Devlin, John, *The Baath Party: A History from Its Origins to 1966*, Stanford, CA: Hoover Institution Press, 1976; and Torrey, Gordon, 'The Baath Ideology and Practice', *Middle East Journal*, 23 (Autumn 1969), pp. 445–70.

4. The following excerpts were taken from an article published by the late and famous Kurdish scholar Ismet Cheriff Vanly, in Ahmed, Mohammed M. A. and Michael M. Gunter (eds), 'The Oppression of the Kurdish people in Syria', *Kurdish Exodus: From Internal Displacement to Diaspora*, Sharon, MA: Ahmed Foundation for Kurdish Studies, 2001, pp. 55–6. The page numerals in the text above refer to those in the actual Hilal manuscript which totalled 160 pages. For a full copy of this lengthy report, see Mella, Jawad, *The Colonial Policy of the Syrian Baath Party in Western Kurdistan*, London: Western Kurdistan Association, 2006, pp. 63–267 and the extended critical replies that follow. Hilal subsequently served as minister of supplies from 1964 to 1970.

5. Tejel, *Syria's Kurds*, pp. 28–9.

6. On these points, see Jwaideh, Wadie, *The Kurdish National Movement: Its Origins and Development*, Syracuse: Syracuse University Press, 2006, p. 145.

7. For further analysis of these issues, see Malanczuk, Peter, *Akehurst's Modern Introduction to International Law*, 7th revised ed., London and New York: Routledge, 1997, pp. 169, 215.

8. Tejel, *Syria's Kurds*, p. 43.

9. Another difference was that no Kurdish party in Syria ever adopted an Islamist doctrine as has occurred in Turkey and Iraq. Alawite rule in Syria and the perceived Kurdish need to co-operate with it is probably one main reason for this position.

10. Sinclair, Christian and Sirwan Kajjo, 'The evolution of Kurdish politics in Syria', *Middle East Research and Information Project*, 31 August 2011. http://www.merip.org/mero/mero083111?p., last accessed 28 July 2013.

11. Tejel, *Syria's Kurds*, p. 89.

12. For more on the multitude of Kurdish political parties in Syria, see KurdWatch, 'Who is the Syrian-Kurdish Opposition? The Development of Kurdish Parties, 1956–2011', Berlin: European Centre for Kurdish Studies, 2011, which contains a list of fourteen Kurdish parties in Syria on pp. 13–15, including their names in English and Kurdish as well as their leaders; and Tejel, *Syria's Kurds*, pp. 48–9,

85–95, and finally 139–40, which contains a list of 'Kurdish political parties in Syria'. A total of thirteen are listed with their names in Kurdish, Arabic and English as well as their leaders, but only as of around 2008.

3. WOMEN

1. Martin van Bruinessen has ably described the best documented cases of women who became rulers or played other 'manly' roles in Kurdistan. See his 'Matriarchy in Kurdistan? Women Rulers in Kurdish History', *International Journal of Kurdish Studies*, 6 (Fall 1993), pp. 25–39; as well as his updated and expanded 'From Adela Khanum to Leyla Zana: Women as Political Leaders in Kurdish History', in Mojab, Shahrzad (ed.), *Women of a Non-State Nation: The Kurds*, Costa Mesa, Ca: Mazda Publishers, 2001, pp. 95–112.

2. Hassanpour, Amir, *Nationalism and Language in Kurdistan, 1918–1985*, San Francisco: Mellen Research University Press, 1992, is perhaps the major recent study in English of the Kurdish language. Chyet, Michael L., *Kurdish-English Dictionary/Ferhenga Kurmanci-Inglizi*, New Haven and London: Yale University Press, 2003, is perhaps the leading work in its field.

3. Mojab (ed.), *Women of a Non-State Nation: The Kurds*. This book is arguably the definitive scholarly collection of articles in English about Kurdish women. It contains historical, political, legal, social, cultural and linguistic perspectives.

4. Yuksel, Metin, 'The Encounter of Kurdish Women with Nationalism in Turkey', *Middle Eastern Studies*, 42 (2006), pp. 777–802 is a scholarly study of this process.

5. Pope, Nicole, 'Kurdish women in Turkey: double discrimination', *Turkish Review*, 1 May 2013. http://www.turkishreview.org/tr/newsDetail_NewsById.action..., last accessed 20 Aug. 2013.

6. Grabolle-Celiker, Anna, *Kurdish Life in Contemporary Turkey: Migration, Gender and Ethnic Identity*, London and New York: I.B. Tauris, 2013, pp. 179–224.

7. Ibid., p. 175.

8. Ibid., p. 217.

9. Gurbey, Gulistan, 'Internally Displaced Kurds in Turkey with Special Focus on Women and Children', in Ahmed, Mohammed M. A. and Michael M. Gunter (eds), *Kurdish Exodus: From Internal Displacement to Diaspora*, Sharon, MA.: Ahmed Foundation for Kurdish Studies, 2002, pp. 3–23. Gurbey discusses the lot of Kurds who were Internally Displaced Persons in Turkey with special attention to the situation of women and children, and considers the causes and consequences of the situation such as housing, employment, health and educational problems.

10. Hardi, Choman, *Gendered Experiences of Genocide: Anfal Survivors in Kurdistan-Iraq*, Farnham, UK: Ashgate, 2011, p. 63.

11. The following discussion is largely based on Gelie, Alessandra and Kerim Yildiz, *Development in Syria: A Gender and Minority Perspective*, London: Kurdish Human Rights Project, 2005, pp. 7–11.

12. Ibid., p. 11.
13. Ibid., p. 90.
14. Kurdish Human Rights Project, *Enforcing the Charter for the Rights and Freedoms of Women in the Kurdish Regions and Diaspora*, London: Kurdish Human Rights Project, 2004.

4. TRANSNATIONAL ACTORS

1. Tejel, Jordi, *Syria's Kurds: History, Politics and Society*, London and New York: Routledge, 2009, p. 5.
2. Hemming, Jon, 'Kurd militants threaten Turkey if it enters Syria', *Reuters*, 22 March 2012, http://www.reuters.com/article/2012/03/22..., last accessed 22 July 2013.
3. Lang, Jennifer, 'Turkey's counterterrorism response to the Syrian crisis', *Terrorism Monitor*, 11, 14 (12 July 2013), http://www.refworld.org..., last accessed 22 July 2013.
4. Idiz, Semih, 'Turkey's Syria policy in shambles over support for Jihadists', *Al-Monitor*, 23 July 2013, http://www.al.monitor.com..., last accessed 25 July 2013.
5. 'Turkey warns Syrian PYD against seeking autonomy', *Today's Zaman*, 20 July 2013, http://www.todayszaman.com..., last accessed 22 July 2013.
6. 'The Kurds should not be left out of the opposition', *Sabah* (Turkey), 26 July 2013, http://www.sabahenglish.com/world..., last accessed 26 July 2013.
7. Ibid.
8. Tejel, *Syria's Kurds*, p. 24.
9. Randal, Jonathan C., *After Such Knowledge, What Forgiveness: My Encounters with Kurdistan*, New York: Farrar, Straus and Giroux, 1997, p. 188.
10. Tejel, *Syria's Kurds*, p. 23.
11. Ibid., p. 18.
12. Ibid., p. 50.
13. Ibid., p. 20.
14. Imset, Ismet G., 'PKK in Syria: burden for Ocalan, trouble for Turkey', *Turkish Daily News* Ankara, 11 November 1993. Also see Imset, Ismet G., *The PKK: A Report on Separatist Violence in Turkey (1973–1992)*, Istanbul: Turkish Daily News Publications, 1992; and Imset, Ismet G., 'The PKK: Terrorists or Freedom Fighters?' *International Journal of Kurdish Studies*, 10, 1 & 2 (1996), pp. 45–100. At the time Imset, a Turkish journalist, was clearly the most knowledgeable source on the PKK. However, he was forced into exile in 1995 when his life was threatened and he ceased his writing. More recently on the PKK, see White, Paul, *Primitive Rebels or Revolutionary Modernizers? The Kurdish National Movement in Turkey*, London and New York: Zed Books, 2000; Ozcan, Ali Kemal, *Turkey's Kurds: A Theoretical Analysis of the PKK and Abdullah Ocalan*, London and New York: Routledge, 2006; Marcus, Aliza, *Blood and Belief: The PKK and the Kurdish Fight for Independence*, New York and London: New York University Press, 2007; Casier,

Marlies and Joost Jongerden (eds), *Nationalism and Politics in 'Turkey: Political Islam, Kemalism and the Kurdish Issue*, London and New York: Routledge, 2011, particularly the two chapters by Joost Jongerden and Ahmet Hamdi Akkaya on the PKK, pp. 123–62; and Unal, Mustafa Cosar, *Counterterrorism in Turkey: Policy Choices and Policy Effects toward the Kurdistan Workers' Party (PKK)*, London and New York: Routledge, 2012, among many others.

15. Montgomery (Allsopp), Harriet, *The Kurds of Syria: An Existence Denied*, Berlin: Europäisches Zentrum für kurdische Studien, 2005, p. 134.
16. Ibid.
17. Tejel, Jordi, *Syria's Kurds*, p. 135.
18. Ibid., p. 123. The Yekiti party also played a leading role in the Qamishli uprising.
19. Ibid., pp. 122 and 137.
20. Brandon, James, 'The PKK and Syria's Kurds', *Terrorism Monitor*, 5, 3 (21 February 2007), pp. 4–6, http://www.jamestown.org..., last accessed 25 July 2013. A PKK member who recently surrendered to Turkish authorities claimed that, 'Syrians constitute the largest number of new PKK recruits.' 'Ongoing civil war in Syria increases recruits for terrorist PKK', *Zaman* (Turkey), 25 July 2013, http://www.todayszaman.com/news..., last accessed 26 July 2013.
21. 'Salih Muslim's press conference before going to Istanbul'.
22. There exists an enormous literature on the Iraqi Kurds. For a brief sample, see Ghareeb, Edmund, *The Kurdish Question in Iraq*, Syracuse: Syracuse University Press, 1981; Gunter, Michael M., *The Kurdish Predicament in Iraq*, New York: St. Martin's Press, 1999; O'Leary, Brendan, John McGarry and Khaled Salih (eds), *The Future of Kurdistan in Iraq*, Philadelphia: University of Pennsylvania Press, 2005; Anderson, Liam and Gareth Stansfield, *Crisis in Kirkuk*, Philadelphia: University of Pennsylvania Press, 2009; Bengio, Ofra, *The Kurds of Iraq: Building a State within a State*, Boulder and London: Lynne Rienner Publishers, 2012; and the relevant parts of McDowall, David, *A Modern History of the Kurds*, London and New York: I.B. Tauris, 1996; Natali, Denise, *The Kurds and the State: Evolving National Identity in Iraq, Turkey, and Iran*, Syracuse: Syracuse University Press, 2005; and Romano, David, *The Kurdish Nationalist Movement: Opportunity, Mobilization and Identity*, Cambridge: Cambridge University Press, 2006, among others.
23. Cited in Landis, J. and J. Pace, 'The Syrian Opposition', *The Washington Quarterly*, 30, 1 (2006–2007), p. 53.
24. KurdWatch, 'Who is the Syrian-Kurdish Opposition? The Development of Kurdish Parties, 1956–2011', Report 8, Berlin: European Centre for Kurdish Studies, 2011, p. 7.
25. The elder Barzani too had earlier played the same game with Iran. In this latter case, Barzani had surrendered Iranian Kurds to Iran—where in some cases they were then executed—in return for Iranian aid to his KDP.
26. Zoepf, Katherine, 'After decades as nonpersons, Syrian Kurds may soon be recognized', *New York Times*, 28 April 2005, http://www.nytimes.com/2005/04/28...,

last accessed 29 July 2013. In English, *Ey Raqip* translates as 'Hey enemy', with the added implication that the Kurds are still surviving and on guard.

5. THE KRG MODEL

1. There exists an enormous literature on the Iraqi Kurds. For a brief sample, see Chapter 4 on 'Transnational Actors,' endnote 22. I previously published portions of this chapter in 'Economic Opportunities in Iraqi Kurdistan', *Middle East Policy*, 18 (Summer 2011), pp. 102–9; and 'Canvassing the Kurdish spring', in Ahmed, Mohammed M. A. and Michael M. Gunter (eds), *The Kurdish Spring: Geopolitical Changes and the Kurds*, Costa Mesa, CA: Mazda Press, 2013, pp. 3–36.

2. For background, see Kurdistan Regional Government, *The Kurdistan Region: Invest in the Future*, Washington, DC: Newsdesk Media Inc., 2007; and Samuel Ciszuk, a Middle East energy analyst with IHS Global Insight in London at www.globalinsight.com. For additional background, see Natali, Denise, *The Kurdish Quasi-State: Development and Dependency in Post-Gulf War Iraq*, Syracuse: Syracuse University Press, 2010.

3. The following data and citations were taken from 'Iraq: oil and gas rights of regions and governorates', KurdishMedia.com, 14 June 2006. With an estimated 1.5 million inhabitants, Irbil is the largest city in the KRG.

4. The following data were taken from Holland, Ben, 'An oil boomtown in Iraqi Kurdistan: Erbil is prospering, but tensions with Baghdad are increasing', *BusinessWeek*, 21 January 2010.

5. Loney, Jim, 'Iraqi Kurdistan crude output about 80,000 bpd', *Reuters*, 18 February 2011, http://af.reuters.com/articles/energyOilNews/idAFLDE71H1OS20110218, last accessed 19 Feb. 2011.

6. 'Iraq to resume Kurdish oil exports soon', *Medyanews*, 9 February 2011, http://medyanews.com/english/?p=747, last accessed 12 Feb. 2011.

7. This and the following data are largely taken from Loney, Jim, 'Snap analysis: big challenges ahead for new Iraq government', *Reuters*, 21 December 2010, http://www.reuters.com/articles/idUSTRE6BK3CZ20101221, last accessed 23 Dec. 2010. Sceptical analysts argue that 6–7 million bpd is actually a more realistic target. El Gamal, Rania and Barbara Lewis, 'Shahristani, architect of Iraq's oil future', *Reuters*, 18 December 2010, http://www.reuters.com/article/id USTRE6 BH0OL20101218?pageNumber=1, last accessed 23 Dec. 2010.

8. 'Iraq oil revenue plan prompts Kurds parl't walkout', *Reuters*, 18 December 2010, http://af.reuters.com/article/energyOilNews/idAFLDE6BH06Y20101218, last accessed 23 Dec. 2010. In January 2011, Kawa Mahmud, a spokesman for the KRG, claimed that an agreement between the KRG and the new al-Maliki government had provided for the Kurdish region to begin oil exports again in early February 2011. Ajrash, Kadhim and Nayla Razzouk, 'Kurdistan to resume crude oil exports early February, KRG spokesman says', Bloomberg.com, 18 January 2011, http://www.bloomberg.com/news/2011–01–18/kurdistan-to…, last accessed

19 Jan. 2011. By the end of March 2011, approximately 115,000 bpd were being pumped for export. Rassouk, Nayla, 'Kurdistan PM expects Iraq to start paying foreign companies', Bloomberg.com, 11 April 2011, http://www.bloomberg.com/news/2011–04–11…, last accessed 14 Apr. 2011.

9. 'Kurdistan's oil and Iraq's new government', *Rudaw*, 6 January 2011, http://rudaw.net/english/science/editorial/3399.html, last accessed 11 Jan. 2011.

10. The following discussion is largely based on Hafidh, Hassan and Angus McDowall, 'Update: Iraqi Kurds: oil laws by June 2011 or won't join government', *Zawya*, 30 November 2010, http://www.zawya.com/Story.cfm/sidZW20101130000084/Iraqi%20Kurds%3A%20Oil%2…, last accessed 3 Dec. 2010.

11. The following data and citation were taken from 'RWE signs regional gas agreement with Kurdistan to help to develop network', MESOP.de, 28 November 2010, http://www.MESOP@online.de, last accessed 29 Nov. 2010.

12. This and the following data were gleaned from 'Erbil ranked 5th for foreign direct investment', *Iraq-Business News*, 17 March 2011, http://www.iraq-businessnews.com/2011/03/16/erbil-ranked-5th…, last accessed 18 Mar. 2011.

13. The following data were largely garnered from Schute Jr., Harry, 'Missed business opportunity in Kurdistan: Turks, Iranians, and Jordanians invest while we sit on sidelines', *Washington Times*, 2 December 2010, http://www.washingtontimes.com/news/2010/dec/2/missed-business-opportunity-in-kurdis…, last accessed 4 Dec. 2010. These annual international fairs have continued through 2013 and also taken place in London.

14. Irbil International Airport was opened in the autumn of 2005 and a new, modern airport began operations in 2010. Constructed by Makyol Cengiz of Turkey, it cost at least $500 million. This new airport has one of the longest runways in the world (4,800 x 75 metres) owing to US military needs, and has scheduled flights to several airports in the Middle East and Europe. Sulaymaniya, the second largest city in the Kurdish region, also has a new but smaller international airport.

15. Aqraqi, Shamal, 'Turkey's Erdogan in first visit to Iraq Kurd region', *Reuters*, 29 March 2011, http://www.reuters.com/article/2011/03/29…, last accessed 4 Apr. 2011.

16. El Gamal, Rania, 'Turkey, Iran battle for clout, deals in Iraq', *Reuters*, 8 December 2010, http://af.reuters.com/article/energyOilNews/idAFLDE6B20LL20101208, last accessed 24 Dec. 2010.

17. This and the following data and citation were garnered from Shadid, Anthony, 'Resurgent Turkey flexes its muscles around Iraq', *New York Times*, 4 January 2011.

18. 'President Barzani and Prime Minister Erdogan open Erbil International Airport and Turkish Consulate', Kurdistan.org, 30 March 2011, http://www.krg.org/articles/detail.asp?, last accessed 31 Mar. 2011.

19. 'Turkish lender excited to open branch in northern Iraq, official says', *Hurriyet Daily News & Economic Review*, 4 December 2010, http://www.hurriyetdailynews.com/n.php?n=turkish-lender-excited…, last accessed 22 Dec. 2010.

20. The following discussion is largely based on Salihi, Mariwan F., 'Foreign investment leads to more shopping malls in Arbil', Gulfnews.com, 30 November 2010, http://Kurdistankorea.blogspot.com/2010/12foreign-investments…, last accessed 22 Dec. 2010. Majidi Mall is named for the prominent Majidi family which owns it.

21. 'The top 41 places to go in 2011', *New York Times*, 9 January 2011, p. 11. Michelle Higgins wrote the short vignette on Iraqi Kurdistan.

22. '20 best trips of 2011', National Geographic website, http://travel.nationalgeographic.com/travel/best-trips-2011-photos/, last accessed 25 Mar. 2011.

23. Cited in Salaheddin, Sinan, 'Iraq's oil expansion plans face major challenges', Post-gazette.com, 15 January 2011, http://www.post-gazette.com/pg/11015/1118208–82.stm?cmpid=nationworld.xml, last accessed 19 Jan. 2011.

24. The following data are taken from Ditz, Jason, 'Emergency parliament session: Iraqi Kurdistan scrambles over protests', MESOP.de, 22 February 2011, http://mesop@online.de, last accessed 22 February 2011; and Tawfeeq, Mohammed, 'Teenager dies, 39 hurt in fresh clashes in Iraq's Kurdistan', *CNN*, 21 February 2011, http://edition.cnn.com/2011/WORLD/meast/02/21/iraq.protests/, last accessed 22 Feb. 2011.

25. 'Reporters without borders documentation: the KRG harassment against journalists', MESOP.de, 21 February 2011, http://www.mesop.de/2011/02/22/…, last accessed 22 Feb. 2011.

26. Cited in Tawfeeq, 'Teenager dies, 39 hurt in fresh clashes'.

27. 'Massoud Barzani calls for Iraqi Kurdistan reforms', Ekurd.net, 3 March 2011, http://www.ekurd.net/mismas/articles/misc2011/3/state4879.htm, last accessed 25 Mar. 2011.

28. For background, see Gunter, Michael M., 'Arab-Kurdish Relations and the Future of Iraq', *Third World Quarterly*, 32, 9 (2011), pp. 1623–35.

29. For further analysis, see Bengio, Ofra, 'Will the Kurds get their way?' *American Interest*, November/December 2012, http://www.mesop.de/2012/10/22/ofra-negio-moshe-dayan-center-will-the-kurds-get-their-way/, last accessed 22 Oct. 2012.

30. For more background, see Chomani, Kamal and Jake Hess, 'Pro-democracy demonstrations in northern Iraq/south Kurdistan', MESOP.de, 2 March 2011, http://www.mesop.de/2011/03/02/pro-democracy…, last accessed 3 Mar. 2011; and Hassan, Kawa, 'South Kurdistan 2011: massive political and social energies: no fundamental changes', *Kurdistan Tribune*, 6 February 2011, http://kurdistan-tribune.com, last accessed 5 June 2012.

31. Cited in Parasiliti, Andrew, 'Barham Salih: Bashar's days are numbered', *Al Monitor*, 12 September 2012, http://www.mesop.de/2012/09/13/barham-salih-bashars…., last accessed 13 Sep. 2012.

32. 'Iraqi Kurdistan President Massoud Barzani seeks right to self-determination', Ekurd.net, 11 December 2011, http://www.ekurd.net/mismas/articles…, last accessed 5 June 2012.

33. For more background on this simmering conflict, see International Crisis Group,

'Iraq and the Kurds: the High-Stakes Hydrocarbons Gambit', Middle East Report No. 120, 19 April 2012.

34. 'US Senator McCain expects Iraq gov't to collapse and split into three different states', Ekurd.net, 11 January 2012, http://www.ekurd.net/mismas/articles..., last accessed 5 June 2012.

35. Biden Joseph R., and Leslie H. Gelf, 'Unity through autonomy in Iraq', *New York Times*, 1 May 2006.

36. Malone, Barry, 'Iraq calls Turkey "Hostile State" as relations dim', *Reuters*, 20 April 2012, http://www.reuters.com/article/2012/04/21/us-iraq-turkey-id..., last accessed 5 June 2012.

37. For further background, see Bengio, Ofra, 'Turkey: a midwife for a Kurdish state?' *Jerusalem Post*, 12 June 2012.

38. 'Kurdistan's Barzani suggests Iraq might use F-16s against Kurds', Ekurd.net, 9 April 2012, http://www.ekurd.net/mismas/articles..., last accessed 5 June 2012.

39. Jakes, Lara, 'Iraq's Kurdistan President Massoud Barzani hints at secession', Ekurd.net, 25 April 2012, http://www.ekurd.net/mismas/articles..., last accessed 5 June 2012.

40. 'Before a full-blown war?' Aswataliraq.ingo, 22 November 2012, http://www.mesop.de/2012/11/22/before-a-full-blown, last accessed 24 Nov. 2012.

6. THE PKK MODEL

1. Earlier uprisings occurred in the 1920s and 1930s. See Olson, Robert, *The Emergence of Kurdish Nationalism and the Sheikh Said Rebellion, 1880–1925*, Austin: University of Texas Press, 1989; and McDowall, David, *A Modern History of the Kurds*, 3rd revised ed., London: I.B. Tauris, 2004. In addition, several legal pro-Kurdish parties have existed since the early 1990s. Although they have been eventually banned by the Turkish government, they too have played a role in what are, in effect, negotiations. See Watts, Nicole F., *Activists in Office: Kurdish Politics and Protest in Turkey*, Seattle: University of Washington Press, 2010. I previously published portions of this chapter as 'Reopening Turkey's Closed Kurdish Opening?' *Middle East Policy*, 20 (Summer 2013), pp. 88–98.

2. For more on these earlier, missed opportunities to find a solution, see Barkey, Henri J. and Graham E. Fuller, 'Turkey's Kurdish Question: Critical Turning Points and Missed Opportunities', *Middle East Journal*, 51 (Winter 1997), pp. 59–79.

3. For more on this topic, see Gunter, Michael M., 'The Continuing Kurdish Problem in Turkey after Ocalan's Capture', *Third World Quarterly*, 21 (October 2000), pp. 849–69.

4. For recent analyses of the Kurdish problem in Turkey, see Unal, Mustafa Cosar, *Counterterrorism in Turkey: Policy Choices and Policy Effects toward the Kurdistan Workers' Party (PKK)*, London and New York: Routledge, 2012; Casier, Marlies and Joost Jongerden (eds), *Nationalisms and Politics in Turkey: Political Islam,*

Kemalism and the Kurdish Issue, London and New York: Routledge, 2011; Gunter, Michael M., *The Kurds Ascending: The Evolving Solution to the Kurdish Problem in Iraq and Turkey*, 2nd ed.; New York: Palgrave Macmillan, 2011; and Marcus, Aliza, *Blood and Belief: The PKK and the Kurdish Fight for Independence*, New York: New York University Press, 2007, among others. In addition, see the proceedings of the 9th annual international conference of the EU Turkey Civic Commission (EUTCC), 'The Kurdish question in Turkey: time to renew the dialogue and resume direct negotiations', 5–6 December 2012, European Parliament, Brussels, Belgium. For some of these proceedings, see http://www.mesop.de.

5. For recent scholarly work on the AK Party (AKP), see Cizre, Umit (ed.), *Secular and Islamic Politics in Turkey: The Making of the Justice and Development Party*, London: Routledge, 2007; Hale, William and Ergun Ozbudun, *Islamism, Democracy and Liberalism in Turkey: The Case of the AKP*, New York: Routledge, 2010; and Yavuz, M. Hakan, *Secularism and Muslim Democracy in Turkey*, New York: Cambridge University Press, 2009. Also see Gunter, Michael M. and M. Hakan Yavuz, 'Turkish Paradox: Progressive Islamists versus Reactionary Secularists', *Critique: Critical Middle Eastern Studies*, 16 (Fall 2007), pp. 289–301.

6. Cited in 'Gul: Kurdish problem is the most important problem of Turkey', *Today's Zaman*, 11 May 2009, http://www.todayszaman.com…, last accessed 4 June 2012.

7. Cited in *Today's Zaman*, 12 August 2009. Also see Casier, Marlies, Joost Jongerden and Nic Walker, 'Fruitless Attempts? The Kurdish Initiative and Containment of the Kurdish Movement in Turkey', *New Perspectives on Turkey*, 44 (Spring 2011), pp. 103–27.

8. Author's contacts with Kurdish sources in Europe and the Middle East. Also see Candar, Cengiz, 'The Kurdish Question: The Reasons and Fortunes of the 'Opening', *Insight Turkey*, 11 (Fall 2009), pp. 13–9.

9. *Hurriyet*, issues of 18 November 2009; 2 December 2009; 9 December 2009; and 14 December 2009; as cited in Cinar, Menderes, 'The Militarization of Secular Opposition in Turkey', *Insight Turkey*, 12 (Spring 2010), p. 119. Also see Keyman, E. Fuat, 'The CHP and the "Democratic Opening": Reactions to AK Party's Electoral Hegemony', *Insight Turkey*, 12 (Spring 2010), pp. 91–108.

10. Celep, Odul, 'Turkey's Radical Right and the Kurdish Issue: The MHP's Reaction to the "Democratic Opening"', *Insight Turkey*, 12 (Spring 2010), p. 136.

11. Cakir, Rusen, 'Kurdish Political Movement and the "Democratic Opening"', *Insight Turkey*, 12 (Spring 2010), p. 185.

12. Actually, despite the government's Kurdish Opening, arrests of Kurdish politicians and notables associated with the Koma Civaken Kurdistan (KCK) or Kurdistan Communities Union, an umbrella PKK organisation supposedly acting as the urban arm of the PKK, had been occurring since 14 April 2009 in apparent retaliation for the DTP local election victories at the end of March 2009. These DTP gains were largely at the expense of the AKP.

13. For further background, see Casier, Marlies, Andy Hilton and Joost Jongerden,

'"Road Maps" and roadblocks in Turkey's southeast', *Middle East Report Online*, http://www.merip.org/mero/mero103009, 30 October 2009.

14. 'Resolution of the Tenth General Assembly Meeting of the Kurdistan National Congress KNK', Brussels, Belgium, 24 May 2010.

15. Wilson, Ross, 'Turkish election: an AKP victory with limits', New Atlanticist: Policy and Analysis Blog, 13 June 2011, http://www.acus.org/new_atlanticist/turkish-election-akp-victory-limits, last accessed 2 Sep. 2011.

16. 'Kurds make big gains in Turkish election', *Today's Zaman*, 13 June 2011, http://www.todayszaman.com/news-247215-kurds-make-big-gains…, last accessed 3 Sep. 2011.

17. Kemal, Lale, 'Turkey's paradigm shift on Kurdish question and KCK trial', *Today's Zaman*, 21 October 2010, which refers to 'state contacts with the imprisoned leader of the PKK, Abdullah Ocalan, on supposedly broader issues', http:///www.todayszaman.com/columnist-224988-turkeys-paradism-shift-on-kurdish-ques…, last accessed 26 Nov. 2010; and Khoshnaw, Hemin, 'Mediator confirms Turkey is negotiating with Ocalan', *Rudaw*, 10 August 2011. http://www.rudaw.net/english/news/turkey/3883.html, last accessed 12 Aug. 2011. More recently, see Khoshnaw, Hemin, 'North Kurdistan (Turkey): secret talks reported between Turkey and imprisoned PKK leader', *Rudaw*, 11 July 2012, http://www.mesop.de/2012/07/11/north-kurdistan-turkey-secret-talks…, last accessed 11 June 2012. This latter article states that, 'the English are mediating between the PKK and MIT [Turkish National Intelligence Organization]', and also refers to the intermediary roles of Leyla Zana (see below) and Ilhami Isik (Balikci).

18. For background, see Hess, Jake, 'The AKP's "New Kurdish Strategy" is nothing of the sort: an interview with Selahattin Demirtas [co-president of the BDP]', Middle East Research and Information Project, 2 May 2012, http://merip.org/mero/mero050212?ip_login_no_cache=…, last accessed 3 May 2012.

19. See, for example, Ocalan, Abdullah, *Declaration on the Democratic Solution of the Kurdish Question*, London: Mesopotamian Publishers, 1999.

20. Ocalan, Abdullah, *Prison Writings: The PKK and the Kurdish Question in the 21st Century*, trans. and edited by Happel, Klaus, London: Transmedia Publishing Ltd., 2011; and Ocalan, Abdullah, *Prison Writings III: The Road Map to Negotiations*, trans. by Guneser, Havin, Cologne: International Initiative Edition, 2012. Also see Uslu, Emre, 'PKK's strategy and the European Charter of Local Self-Government', *Today's Zaman*, 28 June 2010, http://www.todayszaman.com/news-214416–109-pkks-strategy-and-the-european-charter-…, last accessed 26 Nov. 2010.

21. 'Turkey's henchmen in Syrian Kurdistan are responsible for the unrest here', KurdWatch, 8 November 2011, http://www.kurdwatch.org…, last accessed 6 June 2012.

22. Karabat, Ayse, 'Kurds expect Gul's Diyarbakir visit to ease recent tension', *Today's Zaman*, 29 December 2010, http://www.todayszaman.com/news-230981…, last accessed 30 Dec. 2010.

23. Tait, Robert, 'Turkey's military strikes could herald closure for Kurdish opening', RFE/RL, 24 August 2011, http://www.rferl.org/content/turkish_offensive_could_close_kurdish_opening/24307002.ht…, last accessed 29 Aug. 2011.
24. 'Turkey prepares for ground assault on Kurdish rebels in Iraq', *Deutsche Welle*, 24 August 2011, http://www.dw-world.de/dw/article/0,,15342116,00.html, last accessed 29 Aug. 2011. The PKK killed nearly forty Turkish soldiers beginning in July 2011, claiming its attacks were in retaliation for earlier government special forces operations that had killed more than twenty rebels.
25. Fraser, Suzan, 'Turkey says it killed 100 Kurdish rebels in Iraq', *Associated Press*, 23 August 2011, http://cnsnews.com/news/article…, last accessed 29 Aug. 2011.
26. Uslu, Emre, 'The Daglica attack: what does it tell us?' *Today's Zaman*, 20 June 2012, http://www.todayszaman.com/columnist-284160…, last accessed 16 July 2012.
27. The following discussion and citations are taken from Eissenstat, Howard, 'A war on dissent in Turkey', Human Rights Now, 4 November 2011, http://blog.amnestyusa.org/waronterror…, last accessed 13 November 2011.
28. 'Leyla Zana stands by Erdogan remarks in spite of BDP reaction', *Today's Zaman*, 15 June 2012, http://www.todayszaman.com/news-283606…, last accessed 18 June 2012.
29. 'Zana reveals details of Erdogan meeting', *Hurriyet Daily News*, 1 July 1 2012, http://www.hurriyetdailynews.com/zana…, last accessed 13 July 2012.
30. Human Rights Watch, 'Turkey: arrests expose flawed justice system', 1 November 2011, http://www.hrw.org/news/2011/11/01/turkey-arrests-expose…, last accessed 13 Nov. 2011.
31. For background, see Gunter, Michael M., 'Turkey: The Politics of a New Democratic Constitution', *Middle East Policy*, 19 (Spring 2012), pp. 119–25.
32. Human Rights Watch, 'Turkey: arrests expose flawed justice system'. Meral Danis Bestas, the vice-chair of the BDP, told me on 16 May 2012 when I spoke with her through a translator in London that more than 6,000 people had been detained by the Turkish authorities.
33. This and the following data were garnered from Donmez, Ahmet and Aydin Albayrak, 'Government to put together a new roadmap on Kurdish issue', *Zaman*, 22 October 2012, http://www.mesop.ed/2012/10/22/government-to-put-together…, last accessed 23 Oct. 2012.
34. This and the following citation as well at the related discussion are taken from Seibert, Thomas, 'Erdogan calls for unity between Turks and Kurds', *The National*, 24 October 2012, http://www.thenational.ae/news/world/europe…, last accessed 25 Oct. 2012.
35. Yetkin, Murat, 'A rare chance in the Kurdish problem', *Hurriyet Daily News* (Turkey), 7 January 2013, http;//www.hurriyetdailynews.com/a-rare-chance…., last accessed 14 Jan. 2013.
36. Bilefsky, Dan and Alan Cowell, '3 Kurds are killed in Paris in locked-door mystery', *New York Times*, 10 January 2013, http://www.nytimes.com/2013/01/11/

world/europe/three-kurdish-activists-killed-in-central-paris.html?pagewanted=all&_r=0, last accessed 16 Jan. 2013. At time of writing (August 2013) the Parisian police had a suspect under arrest, but it still was not clear if he was guilty and, if so, what his motives were. For further details, see Gunter, Michael M., 'Murder in Paris: Parsing the Murder of Female PKK Leader', *Militant Leadership Monitor*, 4 (January 2013), pp. 12–13.

37. '100 PKK militants to lay down arms: report', *Hurriyet Daily News*, 29 January 2013, http://www.hurriyetdailynews.com/100-pkk-militants..., last accessed 29 Jan. 2013; and 'PKK: disarmament & ceasefire in February?', *Hurriyet*, 29 January 2013, http://www.mesop.de/2013/01/29/pkk-disarmament-ceasefire..., last accessed 29 Jan. 2013.

38. The following analysis is largely based on 'PKK leader's letter to Kandil reaches northern Iraq: report', *Hurriyet Daily News*, 28 February 2013, http://www/mesop.de.de/2013/02/28/pkk-leaders-letter..., last accessed 1 Mar. 2013; and Yackley, Ayla Jean, 'Kurdish rebel leader Ocalan airs frustrations in Turkey peace process', *Reuters*, 1 March 2013, http;//www.mesop.de/2013/03/01/Kurdish-rebel-leader..., last accessed 1 Mar. 2013.

39. 'Turkey's Erdogan calls for more support for peace move', *Today's Zaman*, 26 February 2013, http://www.todayszaman.com/news-308165-turkey's-erdogan..., last accessed 1 Mar. 2013.

40. 'Leak of Imrali record sparks controversy over its source', *Hurriyet*, 29 February [sic], 2013,. http://www.mesop.de/2013/02/28/leak-of-imrali-record..., last accessed 1 Mar. 2013.

41. Hakan Fidan became the head of the MIT in May 2010. He is in his mid-forties and has had a considerable amount of experience in the military, intelligence and foreign policy fields. Most recently he was also the head of the Turkish Development and Cooperation Agency which is tasked with implementing development co-operation towards poverty eradication and sustainable development abroad. His undergraduate degree from the University of Maryland, University College, was in management and political science. Subsequently he earned an MA and PhD from Bilkent University in Ankara. His doctoral dissertation was entitled, 'The Role of Information Technologies in Verifying International Agreements in the Age of Information'.

42. Cited in Traynor, Ian and Constanze Letsch, 'Locked in a fateful embrace: Turkey's PM and his Kurdish prisoner', *The Guardian*, 1 March 2013, http://www.guardian.co.uk/world/2013/mar/01/turkey-pm-kurdish-prisoner-peace..., last accessed 1 Mar. 2013.

43. The following data were taken from Traynor, Ian, 'Turks and Kurds look to good Friday Accords as template for peace', *The Guardian*, 1 March 2013, http://www.guardian.co.uk/world/2013/mar/01/turk-kurd-good-friday-accords..., last accessed 1 Mar. 2013.

44. This and the following citation were gleaned from Simsek, Ayhan, 'EU voices pro peace talks', for *SES Turkiye*, 14 February 2013, http://mesop.de/2013/02/14/eu-voices-pro-peace-talks..., last accessed 14 Feb. 2013.

45. Gursel, Kadri, 'Ocalan negotiations impact/future of Turkish presidency', *Al-Monitor Turkey Pulse*, 1 March 2013, http://www.mesop.de/2013/03/02/ocalan-negotiations-impact-future…, last accessed 1 Mar. 2013.
46. Cited in Traynor, 'Locked in a fateful embrace'.
47. Cited in Yackley, 'Kurdish rebel leader Ocalan airs frustrations in Turkey peace process'.
48. In recognition of this development, the mainline US weekly magazine *Time*, in its issue of 29 April/6 May 2013 named the previously obscure Ocalan as one of 'the 100 most influential people in the world' and called him a 'voice for peace'. Previously, such accolades would have been inconceivable.

7. THE UNITED STATES

1. Baker III, James A. and Lee H. Hamilton (Co-Chairs), *The Iraq Study Group Report: The Way Forward—A New Approach*, New York: Vintage Books, 2006. I originally published portions of this chapter as 'The Five Stages of American Foreign Policy Towards the Kurds', *Insight Turkey*, 13 (Spring 2011), pp. 93–106.
2. Kurdistan Regional Government, 'President Barzani and Defense Secretary Gates in Erbil reaffirm long-term KRG-US relations', 11 December 2009, http://www.krg.org/articles/detail.asp?1ngnr=12&smap=o210100&rnr=223&anr=32969, last accessed 7 Feb. 2011.
3. Lake, Eli, 'U.S. makes political pledge to Kurds in Iraq', *Washington Times*, 16 December 2009.
4. For further background, see Charountaki, Marianna, *The Kurds and US Foreign Policy: International Relations in the Middle East since 1945*, London: Routledge, 2010.
5. See Bemis, Samuel Flagg, *A Diplomatic History of the United States*, 5th ed., New York: Holt, Rinehart and Winston, Inc., 1965, p. 626.
6. On Ataturk and the Turkish War of Independence following the First World War, see Shaw, Stanford J. and Ezel Kural Shaw, *History of the Ottoman Empire and Modern Turkey*, Vol. II, *Reform, Revolution and Republic: The Rise of Modern Turkey, 1808–1975*, Cambridge: Cambridge University Press, 1977, pp. 340–72; Lewis, Bernard, *The Emergence of Modern Turkey*, 2nd ed, London: Oxford University Press, 1968, pp. 239–93; and Zurcher, Erik J., *Turkey: A Modern History*, London: I. B. Tauris, 1994, pp. 138–72.
7. For background, see Edmonds, C. J., *Kurds, Turks and Arabs: Travel and Research in North-Eastern Iraq, 1919–1925*, London: Oxford University Press, 1957.
8. For background, see McDowall, David, *A Modern History of the Kurds*, 3rd ed., London: I. B. Tauris, 2004; and White, Paul, *Primitive Rebels or Revolutionary Modernizers? The Kurdish National Movement in Turkey*, London and New York: Zed Books, 2000.
9. For further background, see Casier, Marlies and Joost Jongerden (eds), *Nationalism and Politics in Turkey: Political Islam, Kemalism and the Kurdish Issue*, London

and New York: Routledge, 2010; Yildiz, Kerim and Susan Breau, *The Kurdish Conflict: International Humanitarian Law and Post-Conflict Mechanisms*, London and New York: Routledge, 2010; and Marcus, Aliza, *Blood and Belief: The PKK and the Kurdish Fight for Independence*, New York and London: New York University Press, 2007.

10. For background, see Ghareeb, Edmund, *The Kurdish Question in Iraq*, Syracuse, NY: Syracuse University Press, 1981; and Gunter, Michael M., *The Kurdish Predicament in Iraq: A Political Analysis*, New York: St. Martin's Press, 1999.

11. Kissinger, Henry, *White House Years*, Boston: Little, Brown and Co., 1979, p. 1265.

12. 'The CIA report the president doesn't want you to read', *Village Voice*, 16 February 1976, pp. 70–92. The part dealing with the Kurds is entitled 'Case 2: arms support', and appears on pp. 85 and 87–8.

13. Korn, David A., 'The Last Years of Mustafa Barzani', *Middle East Quarterly*, 1 (June 1994), pp. 12–27.

14. Randal, Jonathan C., *After Such Knowledge, What Forgiveness? My Encounters with Kurdistan*, New York: Farrar, Straus and Giroux, 1997, p. 299.

15. Cited in 'Iraq: KDP's Barzani urges Arab-Kurdish dialogue', *Al-Majallah* (London), 5–11 October 1997, p. 29, as cited in *Foreign Broadcast Information Service— Near East & South Asia*, 97–283 (10 October 1997), p. 2.

16. The following discussion and citations are taken from the chapter on the 'Kurdish Tragedy' in Kissinger, Henry, *Years of Renewal*, New York: Simon and Schuster, 1999, pp. 576–96.

17. 'Remarks to the American Association for the Advancement of Science', 15 February 1991; cited in *Public Papers of the Presidents of the United States: George Bush, 1991*, vol. 1, Washington: Government Printing Office, 1992, p. 145.

18. Cited in 'United States turns down plea to intervene as Kirkuk falls', *International Herald Tribune*, 30 March 1991.

19. See US Congress, Senate Committee on Foreign Relations, *Civil War in Iraq: A Staff Report to the Committee on Foreign Relations*, by Galbraith, Peter W., 102nd Congress, 1st session, May 1991.

20. Cited in Caglayan, Selim, 'Clinton reprimands Barzani and Talabani', *Hurriyet* (Istanbul), 28 January 1995, p. 18; as cited in *Foreign Broadcast Information Service—West Europe*, 1 February 1995, p. 27.

21. Williams, Katherine A., 'How we lost the Kurdish game', *Washington Post*, 15 September 1996, p. C1.

22. Cited in Weiner, Tim, 'Iraqi offensive into Kurdish zone disrupts US plot to oust Hussein', *New York Times*, 7 September 1996, p. 4.

23. Cited in Fedarko, Kevin, 'Saddam's coup', *Time*, 23 September 1996, p. 44.

24. Cited in Kazaz, Harun, 'Ambiguity surrounds N. Iraq Kurdish Agreement', *Turkish Probe*, 11 October 1998.

25. 'Text: Clinton's report on Iraq's non-Compliance with UN resolutions', *USIS Washington File*, 6 November 1998, GlobalSecurity.org, http://www.globalsecurity.org, last accessed 28 Feb. 2011.

26. 'Ozkok: biggest crisis of trust with US', *Turkish Daily News*, 7 July 2003; and Kralev, Nicholas, 'U.S. warns Turkey against operations in northern Iraq', *Washington Times*, 8 July 2003.

27. See endnote 1.

28. Kurdistan Regional Government, 'President Barzani and Defense Secretary Gates in Erbil Reaffirm long-term KRG-US Relations', 11 December 2009.

29. Ibid.

30. Lake, Eli, 'U.S. makes political pledge to Kurds in Iraq', *Washington Times*, 16 December 2009.

31. For an excellent background on this strategic issue, see Anderson, Liam and Gareth Stansfield, *Crisis in Kirkuk: The Ethnopolitics of Conflict and Compromise*, Philadelphia: University of Pennsylvania Press, 2009.

32. Uslu, Emrullah, 'PKK intensifies violence to bring Turkey into confrontation with the European Union', 8 *Terrorism Monitor*, 8 July 2010, http://www.jamestown.org/programs…, last accessed 1 Mar. 2011.

33. See, for example, US Department of State, Bureau of Democracy, Human Rights, and Labor, *Country Reports on Human Rights Practices—2009*, issued 11 March 2010, http://www.state.gov…, last accessed 1 Mar. 2011.

34. 'Martin Indyk statement, House International Relations Committee, June 8', *Iraq News*, 11 June 1999.

35. Cited in Marshall, Toni, 'Kurds call Turkey hypocritical', *Washington Times*, 9 April 1999.

36. Author interview with officials at the US State Department, Washington, DC, 4 April 1997.

37. The following data were taken from *Briefing* (Ankara), 30 November 1998, p. 16.

38. Cited in *Turkish Daily News*, 25 December 1998.

39. Cited in 'U.S. says Ocalan should be brought to justice', *Reuters*, 1 February 1999.

40. 'Remarks by Ambassador Mark R. Parris to the American-Turkish Council's 18th Annual Conference on U.S.-Turkish Relations', 6 May 1999.

41. Jenkins, Gareth, 'A military analysis of Turkey's incursion into northern Iraq', *Terrorism Monitor*, 6 (7 March 2008), http://www.jamestown.org/programs…, last accessed 1 Mar. 2011.

42. 'US may help Turkey combat Kurdish rebels: Gates', *Agence France Presse*, 6 February 2010, http://www.google.com/hostednews/afp/article…, last accessed 1 Mar. 2011.

43. For background, see US Congress, Senate Committee on Foreign Relations. 'Syria Transition Support Act of 2013', S. Rept. 113–79, 113th Congress, 24 July 2013, http://beta.congress.gov/congressional-report/113th-congress/senate-report/79/1, last accessed 22 Sep. 2013.

44. There are reports that Jordan is serving as a base for the US Central Intelligence Agency, training Syrian rebels with support from Saudi Arabia. Cockburn, Patrick, 'How action over Syria risks unsettling fragile balance of power in the Middle East', *The Independent*, 28 August 2013, http://www.independent.co.uk/voices/commentators/how-action-over…, last accessed 28 Aug. 2013.

45. van Wilgenburg, Wladimar, 'Kurdish party rejects US condemnation of "PYD's deadly response"', *Rudaw*, 2 July 2013, http://rudaw.net/english..., last accessed 18 July 2013; and 'PYD press release: on statement of U.S. Department of State regarding situation in Amuda, Syria', 1 July 2013, http://peaceinkurdisatancampaign.worldpress.co..., last accessed 18 July 2013.

46. 'Salah Muslim's press conference before going to Istanbul', *Transnational Middle East Observer*, 26 July 2013, http://www. mesop.de/2013/07/salih-muslims..., last accessed 26 July 2013.

47. The following citations and discussion are taken from Civiroglu, Mutlu, 'PYD's Salih Muslim: we are awaiting an invitation for talks with Washington', *Rudaw*, 17 August 2013, http://www.mesop.de/2013/08/17/pyds-salih-muslim..., last accessed 17 Aug. 2013.

8. PRELUDE

1. However, the more militant Yekiti (Union) party did favour these demonstrations and earlier had organised protests in Damascus on International Human Rights Day on 10 December 2002, and World Children's Day on 25 June 2003. The PKK-affiliated PYD also supported the *Serhildan*. However, both parties ceased active support once the regime had gained the upper hand by the end of March 2004.

2. See, for example, Lesch, David W., *Syria: The Fall of the House of Asad*, London and New Haven: Yale University Press, 2012; Wieland, Carsten, *Syria: A Decade of Lost Chances: Repression and Revolution from Damascus Spring to Arab Spring*, Seattle: Cune Press, 2012; Lefevre, Raphael, *Ashes of Hama: The Muslim Brotherhood in Syria*, London: Hurst Publishers, 2012; Starr, Stephen, *Revolt in Syria: Eye-Witness to the Uprising*, New York: Columbia University Press, 2012; Haddad, Bassam, *Business Networks in Syria: The Political Economy of Authoritarian Resilience*, Stanford, CA: Stanford University Press, 2012; and Heydemann, Steven and Reinoud Leenders, *Middle East Authoritarianisms: Governance, Contestation and Regime Resilience in Syria and Iraq*, Stanford CA: Stanford, University Press, 2013.

3. For earlier figures, see International Crisis Group, 'Syria's: Metastasizing Conflicts', Middle East Report No. 143, 27 June 2013, p. 1, fn. 1 and 2.

4. Barnard, Anne, 'Syria weighs its tactics as pillars of its economy continue to crumble', *New York Times*, 13 July 2013.

5. Dehglan, Saeed Kamali, 'Syrian army being aided by Iranian forces', *The Guardian*, 28 May 2012, http://www.guardian.co.uk/world/2012/may/28/syria..., last accessed 4 August 2013.

6. Gordon, Michael R., 'Iran supplying Syrian military via Iraqi airspace', *New York Times*, 4 September 2012.

7. Barnard, Anne, 'Leader of Hezbollah warns it is ready to come to Syria's aid', *New York Times*, 30 April 2013.

8. Bitar Karim, Emile, trans. Goulden, Charles, 'Syria: proxy theater of war', *Other*

Voices, 16, 6 (August 2013), pp. OV-3–OV-5. This article originally appeared in *Le Monde Diplomatique*, June 2013.

9. Barry, Ellen and Rick Gladstone, 'Turkish premier says Russian munitions were found on Syrian jet', *New York Times*, 11 October 2012.

10. ICG, 'Syria's metastasizing conflicts', p. 3, fn. 14.

11. Bouckaert, Peter, 'Is this the most disgusting atrocity filmed in the Syrian civil war?' *Foreign Policy*, 13 May 2013, http://www.foreignpolicy.com/articles/2013/05/13/most-disgusting-atrocity..., last accessed 5 Aug. 2013. Of course, the regime has committed its egregious atrocities, such as the massacre of as many as 100 civilians near the city of Baniyas located on the Mediterranean Sea some twenty miles north of Tartus on 3 May 2013. See 'Syrian dictator Assad "Massacres up to 100 men, women and children" with knives and guns as US says arming rebels is now an option', *Daily Mail*, 4 May 2013, http://www.dailymail.co.uk/news/article-2318993/..., last accessed 29 May 2013.

12. Giglio, Mike, 'Syria's Bashar Al-Assad is winning', *The Daily Beast*, 17 May 2013, http://thedailybeast.cheapbabysclothes.co.uk/articles..., last accessed 5 Aug. 2013.

13. Abdulmajid, Adib, 'Leaked files: Kurdish leader Mishaal Tammo was killed by direct order from Assad', *Rudaw*, 17 October 2012, http://www.rudaw.net/english/news/syria/5323.html, last accessed 18 Oct. 2012.

14. 'The murder of Mischa Al-Tammu', Kurdwatch, 15 June 2012, http://www.mesop.de/2012/06/17/the-murder..., last accessed 18 June 2012.

15. Abdulmajid, Adib, 'Violent confrontations between Kurdish groups in Syria', *Rudaw*, 10 June 2012, http://www.rudaw.net/english/news/syria/4825.thml, last accessed 11 June 2012; and 'Shoot out: PYD vs. KNC', *Rudaw*, 17 June 2012, http://www.mesop.de/2012/06/17/shoot-out-pyd-vs-knc, last accessed 18 June 2012.

9. AUTONOMY

1. On 11 May 2013, for example, in what Turkey saw as blowback from Syria for Turkish support of the oppositionists, two bombings killed fifty-one and injured 140 in Reyhanli, a city on the Mediterranean coast just across the Syrian border.

2. Salih Muslim, e-mail reply to Michael Gunter, 10 July 2013.

3. 'Iraq-Syria: as Kurds enter the fray, risk of conflict grows', IRIN: Humanitarian News and Analysis (UN Office for the Coordination of Humanitarian Affairs), 2 August 2012, http://www.irinnews.org/Report/96007/IRAQ-Syria..., last accessed 2 Aug. 2012.

4. Shumilin, Alexander, 'Why Russia will not abandon Assad: the internal dynamics behind Russia's Syria policy', Center for Greater Middle East Conflicts at the Institute for the USA & Canada Studies (Russian Academy of Sciences), 15 August 2012, http://www.mesop.de/2012/08/17/why-russia..., last accessed 17 Aug. 2012.

5. Cited in 'Syrian Kurdish leader: US cannot succeed in the Middle East without

the support of Kurds', Ekurd.net, 20 June 2008, http://www.ekurd.net/mismas/articles/misc2008/6/syriakurdistan142.htm, last accessed 8 June 2013.

6. Hassino, Omar and Ilhan Tanir, 'The decisive minority: the role of Syria's Kurds in the Anti-Assad revolution', a Henry Jackson Society Report, March 2012, http://www.scpss.org/libs/spaw..., last accessed 6 June 2012. Also see Natali, Denise, 'Syrian Kurdish cards', http://sharifbehruz.com..., last accessed 6 June 2012.

7. Uslu, Emrullah, 'How Kurdish PKK militants are exploiting the crisis in Syria...,' *Terrorism Monitor*, 6 April 2012, http://www.jamestown.org/..., last accessed 6 June 2012.

8. Shwany, Nabaz, 'Is that right to accuse the PYD for supporting Bashir Assad...,' Ekurd.net, 7 March 2012, http://www.ekurd.net/mismas/articles..., last accessed 6 June 2012.

9. 'Interview with Salih Muhammad, President of PYD', *Firat News*, February 2012, http://en.firatnews.eu/index.php?..., last accessed 28 Feb. 2012.

10. 'Western powers will support Syrian Kurds: Kurdish leader', Ekurd.net, 6 February 2012, http://www.ekurd.net/mismas/articles..., last accessed 18 Oct. 2013.

11. Pydrojava.net, 12 April 2012.

12. One might note the similarity of this title to that of the PKK's Hezen Parastina Gel (HPG) or Peoples Defence Force.

13. Hartling, Peter, 'Arab rebel-Kurd tensions', Agence France Presse (AFP), 31 October 2012, http://www.mesop.de/2012/10/31/arab-rebel-kurd-tensions..., last accessed 31 Oct. 2012.

14. Salih Muslim emphasised this fact in an e-mail to me dated 10 July 2013.

15. Weiss, Michael, 'The impending Syrian-Kurdish conflict', Now Lebanon, 2 November 2012, http://www.nowlebanon.com/NewsArticleDetails.aspx?ID=453196, last accessed 7 Nov. 2012; and Al-Tamimi, Aymenn Jawad, 'Kurdish rivalries in Syria', *The American Spectator*, 8 November 2012, http://www.meforum.org/3372/kurdish-rivalries-syria, last accessed 8 Nov. 2012.

16. Tejel, Jordi, *Syria's Kurds: History, Politics and Society*, London and New York: Routledge, 2009, pp. 79 and 156/fn. 17.

17. The Kurdish Union (Yekiti) Party, founded in 1992 and often a bitter foe of the PYD, also has some armed units, as do both branches of the Kurdish Freedom (Azadi) Party. In addition, Massoud Barzani's KDP was training some units for the Kurdish Democratic Party of Syria (*el-Parti*), but was shocked at their incompetence. See Savelsberg, Eva and Jordi Tejel, 'The Syrian Kurds in "Transition to Somewhere"', in Ahmed, Mohammed M. A. and Michael M. Gunter (eds), *The Kurdish Spring: Geopolitics Changes and the Kurds*, Costa Mesa, CA: Mazda Publishers, 2013, p. 214. Nevertheless, the PYD/YPG maintains the dominant armed Kurdish militia in Syria.

18. van Wilgenburg, Wladimir, 'Border arrests reveal disunity, conflict among Syrian Kurds', Al-Monitor, 21 May 2013, http://www.al-monitor.com/pulse/originals/2013/05/pyd-arrests-syrian-kurds.html, last accessed 8 Aug. 2013.

19. 'Protests of Kurdish youth against PYD', MESOP, 10 August 2013, http://www. mesop.de/2013/08/09/protests…, last accessed 10 Aug. 2013.

20. KurdWatch, 'Press release: on our own behalf: KurdWatch employee threatened with death', KurdWatch, 13 August 2013, http://www.kurdwatch.org, last accessed 13 Aug. 2013.

21. Salih Muslim, e-mail response to Michael Gunter, 10 July 2013.

22. 'Turkey's henchmen in Syrian Kurdistan are responsible for the unrest here', KurdWatch, 8 November 2011, http://www.kurdwatch.org…, last accessed 6 June 2012.

23. Avci, Ismail, 'PKK allegedly kills another Kurdish politician in Syria', *Today's Zaman*, 28 March 2012, http://www.todayszaman.com…, last accessed 6 June 2012.

24. See, for example, Ocalan, Abdullah, *Declaration on the Democratic Solution of the Kurdish Question*, London: Mesopotamian Publishers, 1999; Ocalan, Abdullah. *Prison Writings: The PKK and the Kurdish Question in the 21st Century*, trans. and edited by Happel Klaus, London: Transmedia Publishing, 2011; and Ocalan, Abdullah, *Prison Writings III: The Road Map to Negotiations*, trans. by Guneser, Havin, Cologne: International Initiative Edition, 2012. Also see Uslu, Emre, 'PKK's strategy and the European Charter of Local Self-Government', *Today's Zaman*, 28 June 2010, http://www.todayszaman.com/news-214416–109-pkks-strategy-and-the-european-charter-…, last accessed 26 Nov. 2010.

25. Cited in 'Turkey's henchmen…', KurdWatch, 8 November 2011.

26. Cited in Ibid.

27. Cited in Pydrojava.net, 12 April 2012.

28. Cited in 'The Kurdish Patriotic Conference is nothing more than a name…', KurdWatch, 21 March 2012, http://kurdwatch.org.html/en/syria…, last accessed 6 June 2012.

29. Arango, Tim, 'Kurds prepare to pursue more autonomy in a fallen Syria', *New York Times*, 28 September 2012; and Al Tamimi, Aymenn, 'Syria's Kurds stand alone after rejecting rebels and regime', *The National*, 23 July 2012, http://www. thenational.ae/thenationalconversation/comment/syrias-kurds…, last accessed 25 June 2012.

30. E-mail interview with Savelsberg, Eva, KurdWatch, European Centre for Kurdish Studies, Berlin, 26 August 2013.

31. 'Al-Nusra commits to al-Qaeda, deny Iraq branch merger', Agence France Presse, 10 April 2013, http://www.naharnet.com/stories/en/78961-al-nusra-commits…, last accessed 10 Aug. 2013.

32. Cited in Sherlock, Ruth, 'Inside Jabhat al Nusra—the most extreme wing of Syria's struggle', *The Daily Telegraph*, 2 December 2012, http://www.telegraph. co.uk/news/worldnews/middleeast/syria/9716545…, last accessed 10 Aug. 2013.

33. Lang, Jennifer, 'Turkey's counterterrorism response to the Syrian crisis', *Terrorism Monitor*, 11, 4 (12 July 2013), http://www.mesop.de/2013/07/13/turkeys-counterterrorism-response…, last accessed 13 June 2013.

34. Faraj, Reina, 'The misogyny of Salafist doctrine', *As-Safir* (Lebanon), 15 April 2013, http://www.al-monitor.com/pulse/culture/2013/04/salafist..., last accessed 9 Aug. 2013.

35. 'PYD announces constitution for Kurdish regions', *Kurdpress*, 22 July 2013, http://www.mesop.de/2013/07/22/pyd-announces..., last accessed 22 June 2013.

36. Cited in Khoshnaw, Hemin, 'Salih Muslim's Ankara visit marks major policy change', *Rudaw*, 29 July 2013, http://rudaw.net/english/middleeast/syria/29072013, last accessed 2 Aug. 2013.

37. Ozerkan, Fulya, 'Turkey softens stance on Syria's emboldened Kurds after launching peace process at home', *The Daily Star* (Lebanon), 7 August 2013, http://www.dailystar.com.lb/News/Analysis/2013/Aug-07/226577-turkey-softens..., last accessed 7 Aug. 2013.

38. This and the following citation were taken from Burch, Jonathan, 'Syrian Kurds take fragile steps toward autonomy', *The Daily Star*, 3 August 2013, http://www.dailystar.com.lb/News/Middle-East/2013/Aug-03/226122-syrian-kurds-take..., last accessed 7 Aug. 2013.

39. 'Iraqi Kurd leader Massoud Barzani issues Syria warning', *BBC News Middle East*, 10 August 2013, http://www.bbc.co.uk/news/world-middle-east-23650894, last accessed 17 Aug. 2013.

10. THE FUTURE

1. Confusingly, an earlier Decree 49 of 10 September 2008 had essentially worked in an opposite direction by making it more difficult for Kurds to hold property. Apparently, every year the Syrian regime begins numbering its decrees with numeral 1 again.

2. Pude, Joseph, 'The Kurds and the future of Syria', http://www.kurdnas.com/en/index.php?option=com_content&view..., last accessed 6 Aug. 2013.

3. This and the following citations in this paragraph were taken from 'Turkey's henchmen in Syrian Kurdistan are responsible for the unrest here', KurdWatch, 8 November 2011, http://www.kurdwatch.org..., last accessed 6 June 2012.

4. This and the following citations and data were largely taken from 'KCK: Turkey behind the attacks on Serekaniye', ANF, 18 July 2013, http://www.mesop.de/2013/07/18/kck-turkey-behind..., last accessed 18 June 2013.

5. Salih Muslim, e-mail to the author, dated 10 July 2013.

6. In his unpublished writings, Ocalan declared that, 'the world view for which I stand is close to that of Bookchin [...] I suggested that Bookchin must be read and his ideas are practiced'. Cited in Jongerden, Joost and Ahmet Hamdi Akkaya, 'Democratic Confederalism as a Kurdish Spring: the PKK and the Quest for Radical Democracy', in Ahmed, Mohammed M. A. and Michael M. Gunter (eds), *The Kurdish Spring: Geopolitical Changes and the Kurds*, Costa Mesa, CA: Mazda Publishers, 2013, p. 176.

7. White, Damian F., *Bookchin: A Critical Appraisal*, London: Pluto Press, 2008, p. 159.

8. Bookchin, Murray, 'Libertarian Municipalism: An Overview', *Green Perspectives*, 24 (1991), p. 11.

9. Ibid., p. 7.

10. Bookchin, Murray, 'The Meaning of Confederalism', *Green Perspectives*, 20 (1990), p. 9.

11. This and the following citation were taken from Ibid., p. 10.

12. Ibid., p. 11.

13. Ibid., p. 10.

14. Ibid., p. 4.

15. Jongerden, Joost and Ahmet Hamdi Akkaya, 'Democratic Confederalism as a Kurdish Spring: the PKK and the Quest for Radical Democracy', in Ahmed, Mohammed M. A. and Michael M. Gunter (eds), *The Kurdish Spring: Geopolitical Changes and the Kurds*, Costa Mesa, CA: Mazda Publishers, 2013, pp. 163–85. See also Akkaya, Ahmet Hamdi and Joost Jongerden, 'Reassembling the Political: the PKK and the Project of Radical Democracy', *European Journal of Turkish Studies* [Online], 14/2012, online since 18 January 2013, http://ejts.revues.org/4615, last accessed 18 April 2013.

16. Bookchin, 'Libertarian Municipalism', p. 3.

17. Bookchin, 'The Meaning of Confederalism', p. 13.

18. Ocalan, *Prison Writings III: The Road Map to Negotiations*, p. 89.

19. Cited in Jonderden and Akkaya, 'Democratic Confederalism as a Kurdish Spring', p. 174.

20. Ocalan, *Prison Writings III*, pp. 93–4. For convenience, the following page numerals in the text refer to this Ocalan book so that repetitious endnotes may be avoided.

21. See Jonderden and Akkaya, 'Democratic Confederalism as a Kurdish Spring', pp. 180–84 for a detailed description of the DTK.

22. 'Kurdish group declares democratic autonomy within Turkey's borders', *Sunday's Zaman*, 14 July 2011, http://www.todayszaman.com/news-250503-kurdish… last accessed 25 July 2013.

23. 'Turkey: arrests expose flawed justice system', Human Rights Watch, 1 November 2011, http://www.hrw.org/news/2011/11/01/turkey-arrests-expose, last accessed 25 Aug. 2013.

24. 'Kurdish National Convention postponed for a second time', *Rudaw*, 5 September 2013, http://rudaw.net/mobile/english/jurdistan/05092013, last accessed 5 Sep. 2013.

BIBLIOGRAPHY

Please consult my extensive endnotes at the end of each chapter for the various, mostly online news and other sources that I have used in this book but not listed in this bibliography.

Abu Jaber, Kamel S., *The Arab Ba'th Socialist Party: History, Ideology, and Organization*, Syracuse: Syracuse University Press, 1966.

Ahmed, Mohammed M. A. and Michael M. Gunter (eds), *The Kurdish Spring: Geopolitical Changes and the Kurds*, Costa Mesa, CA: Mazda Press, 2013.

Akkaya, Ahmet Hamdi and Joost Jongerden, 'Reassembling the political: the PKK and the project of radical democracy', *European Journal of Turkish Studies* [Online], 14/2012, online since 18 January 2013, http://ejts.revues. org/4615, last accessed 18 Apr. 2013.

Allsopp, Harriet, 'The Kurdish Autonomy Bid in Syria: Challenges and Reactions', in Ahmed, Mohammed M. A. and Michael M. Gunter (eds), *The Kurdish Spring: Geopolitics Changes and the Kurds*, Costa Mesa, CA: Mazda Publishers, 2013, pp. 218–49.

———. *The Kurds of Syria: Political Parties and Identity in the Middle East*, London: I. B. Tauris, forthcoming.

Al-Tamimi, Aymenn Jawad, 'Kurdish rivalries in Syria', *The American Spectator*, 8 November 2012, http://www.meforum.org/3372/kurdish-rivalries-syria, last accessed 8 Nov. 2012.

Amnesty International, *Document—Syria: Kurds in the Syrian Arab Republic One Year After the March 2004 Events*, 2005, http://www.amnesty.org/en/library/ asset..., last accessed 26 Sep. 2013.

Anderson, Benedict, *Imagined Communities: Reflections on the Origin and Spread of Nationalism*, London: Verso, 1991.

Anderson, Liam and Gareth Stansfield, *Crisis in Kirkuk: The Ethnopolitics of Conflict and Compromise*, Philadelphia: University of Pennsylvania Press, 2009.

Baker III, James A. and Lee H. Hamilton (Co-Chairs), *The Iraq Study Group Report: The Way Forward—A New Approach*, New York: Vintage Books, 2006.

Barkey, Henri J. and Graham E. Fuller, 'Turkey's Kurdish Question: Critical Turning Points and Missed Opportunities', *Middle East Journal*, 51 (Winter 1997), pp. 59–79.

Behrendt, Gunter, *Nationalismus in Kurdistan: Vorgeschichte, Entstehungsbedingungen und erste Manifestationen bis 1925*, Hamburg: Dt. Orient-Inst., 1993.

Bemis, Samuel Flagg, *A Diplomatic History of the United States*, 5th ed., New York: Holt, Rinehart and Winston, Inc., 1965.

Bengio, Ofra, *The Kurds of Iraq: Building a State Within a State*, Boulder and London: Lynne Rienner Publishers, 2012.

Bitar, Karim Emile, trans. by Charles Goulden, 'Syria: Proxy Theater of War', *Other Voices*, 16, 6 (August 2013), pp. OV-3–OV-5.

Bookchin, Murray, 'Libertarian Muncipalism: An Overview', *Green Perspectives*, No. 24 (1991).

———. 'The Meaning of Confederalism', *Green Perspectives*, No. 20 (1990).

Brandon, James, 'The PKK and Syria's Kurds', *Terrorism Monitor*, 5, 3 (21 February 2007), pp. 4–6, http://www.jamestown.org…, last accessed 25 July 2013.

Bruinessen, Martin van, 'From Adela Khanum to Leyla Zana: Women as Political Leaders in Kurdish History', in Mojab, Shahrzad (ed.), *Women of a Non-State Nation: The Kurds*, Costa Mesa, CA: Mazda Publishers, 2001, pp. 95–112.

———. 'Matriarchy in Kurdistan? Women Rulers in Kurdish History', *International Journal of Kurdish Studies*, 6 (Fall 1993), pp. 25–39.

———. *Agha, Shaikh and State: The Social and Political Structure of Kurdistan*, London and New Jersey: Zed Books, 1992.

Cakir, Rusen, 'Kurdish Political Movement and the "Democratic Opening"', *Insight Turkey*, 12 (Spring 2010), pp. 179–92.

Candar, Cengiz, 'The Kurdish Question: The Reasons and Fortunes of the "Opening"', *Insight Turkey*, 11 (Fall 2009), pp. 13–9.

Casier, Marlies and Joost Jongerden (eds), *Nationalism and Politics in Turkey: Political Islam, Kemalism and the Kurdish Issue*, London and New York: Routledge, 2011.

Casier, Marlies, Joost Jongerden and Nic Walker, 'Fruitless Attempts? The Kurdish Initiative and Containment of the Kurdish Movement in Turkey', *New Perspectives on Turkey*, 44 (Spring 2011), pp. 103–27.

Celep, Odul, 'Turkey's Radical Right and the Kurdish Issue: The MHP's Reaction to the "Democratic Opening"', *Insight Turkey*, 12 (Spring 2010), pp. 125–42.

Charles, Lorraine and Kate Denman, 'Every Knot has Someone to Undo It: Using the Capabilities Approach as a Lens to View the Status of Women Leading up to the Arab Spring in Syria', *Journal of International Women's Studies*, 13, 5 (October 2012), pp. 195–210.

Charountaki, Marianna, *The Kurds and US Foreign Policy: International Relations in the Middle East Since 1945*, London: Routledge, 2010.

Chyet, Michael L., *Kurdish-English Dictionary/Ferhenga Kurmanci-Inglizi*, New Haven and London: Yale University Press, 2003.

Cinar, Menderes, 'The Militarization of Secular Opposition in Turkey', *Insight Turkey*, 12 (Spring 2010), pp. 109–23.

Cizre, Umit (ed.), *Secular and Islamic Politics in Turkey: The Making of the Justice and Development Party*, London: Routledge, 2007.

Connor, Walker, *Ethnonationalism: The Quest for Understanding*, Princeton: Princeton University Press, 1994.

Devlin, John, *The Baath Party: A History from Its Origins to 1966*, Stanford, CA: Hoover Institution Press, 1976.

Edmonds, C. J., *Kurds, Turks and Arabs: Travel and Research in North-Eastern Iraq, 1919–1925*, London: Oxford University Press, 1957.

EU Turkey Civic Commission (EUTCC), 'The Kurdish Question in Turkey: Time to Renew the Dialogue and Resume Direct Negotiations', 5–6 December 2012, European Parliament, Brussels. For some of these proceedings, see http://www.mesop.de.

Fuccaro, Nelida, 'Kurds and Kurdish Nationalism in Mandatory Syria: Politics, Culture and Identity', in Abbas Vali (ed.), *Essays on the Origins of Kurdish Nationalism*, Costa Mesa, CA: Mazda Publishers, 2003, pp. 191–217.

Gelie, Alessandra and Kerim Yildiz, *Development in Syria: A Gender and Minority Perspective*, London: Kurdish Human Rights Project, 2005.

Gellner, Ernest, *Nations and Nationalism*, Ithaca: Cornell University Press, 1983.

Ghareeb, Edmund, *The Kurdish Question in Iraq*, Syracuse: Syracuse University Press, 1981.

Grabolle-Celiker, Anna, *Kurdish Life in Contemporary Turkey: Migration, Gender and Ethnic Identity*, London and New York: I. B. Tauris, 2013.

Gunter, Michael M., 'Murder in Paris: Parsing the Murder of Female PKK Leader', *Militant Leadership Monitor*, 4 (January 2013), pp. 12–3.

———. 'Turkey: The Politics of a New Democratic Constitution', *Middle East Policy*, 19 (Spring 2012), pp. 119–25.

———. *The Kurds Ascending: The Evolving Solution to the Kurdish Problem in Iraq and Turkey*, 2nd ed., New York: Palgrave Macmillan, 2011.

———. 'Arab-Kurdish Relations and the Future of Iraq', *Third World Quarterly*, 32, 9 (2011), pp. 1623–35.

———. 'The Continuing Kurdish Problem in Turkey after Ocalan's Capture', *Third World Quarterly*, 21 (October 2000), pp. 849–69.

———. *The Kurdish Predicament in Iraq*, New York: St. Martin's Press, 1999.

Gunter, Michael M. and M. Hakan Yavuz, 'Turkish Paradox: Progressive Islamists Versus Reactionary Secularists', *Critique: Critical Middle Eastern Studies*, 16 (Fall 2007), pp. 289–301.

Gurbey, Gulistan, 'Internally displaced Kurds in Turkey with Special Focus on Women and Children', in Mohammed M. A. Ahmed and Michael M. Gunter (eds), *Kurdish Exodus: From Internal Displacement to Diaspora*, Sharon, MA: Ahmed Foundation for Kurdish Studies, 2002, pp. 3–23.

Haddad, Bassam, *Business Networks in Syria: The Political Economy of Authoritarian Resilience*, Stanford, CA: Stanford University Press, 2012.

Hale, William and Ergun Ozbudun, *Islamism, Democracy and Liberalism in Turkey: The Case of the AKP*, New York: Routledge, 2010.

Hardi, Choman, *Gendered Experiences of Genocide: Anfal Survivors in Kurdistan-Iraq*, Farnham, UK: Ashgate, 2011.

Hassanpour, Amir, *Nationalism and Language in Kurdistan, 1918–1985*, San Francisco: Mellen Research University Press, 1992.

Hassino, Omar and Ilhan Tanir, 'The decisive minority: the role of Syria's Kurds in the anti-Assad revolution', A Henry Jackson Society Report, March 2012, http://www.scpss.org/libs/spaw…, last accessed 6 June 2012.

Heydemann, Steven and Reinoud Leenders, *Middle East Authoritarianisms: Governance, Contestation and Regime Resilience in Syria and Iraq*, Stanford, CA: Stanford University Press, 2103.

Imset, Ismet G., 'The PKK: Terrorists or Freedom Fighters?', *International Journal of Kurdish Studies*, 10, 1&2 (1996), pp. 45–100.

———. *The PKK: A Report on Separatist Violence in Turkey (1973–1992)*, Istanbul: Turkish Daily News Publications, 1992.

International Crisis Group. 'Syria's Kurds: A Struggle Within a Struggle', Middle East Report No. 136, 22 January 2013.

———. 'Syria's: Metastasizing Conflicts', Middle East Report No. 143, 27 June 2013.

———. 'Iraq and the Kurds: the high-stakes Hydrocarbons Gambit', Middle East Report No. 120, 19 April 2012.

Jenkins, Gareth, 'A military analysis of Turkey's incursion into northern Iraq', *Terrorism Monitor*, 6 (7 March 2008), http://www.jamestown.org/programs…, last accessed 1 Mar. 2011.

Jongerden, Joost and Ahmet Hamdi Akkaya, 'Democratic confederalism as a Kurdish Spring: the PKK and the quest for radical democracy', in Mohammed M. A. Ahmed and Michael M. Gunter (eds), *The Kurdish Spring: Geopolitical Changes and the Kurds*, Costa Mesa, CA: Mazda Publishers, 2013.

Jwaideh, Wadie, *The Kurdish National Movement: Its Origins and Development*, Syracuse N.Y.: Syracuse University Press, 2006.

Keyman, E. Fuat, 'The CHP and the "Democratic Opening": Reactions to AK Party's Electoral Hegemony', *Insight Turkey*, 12 (Spring 2010), pp. 91–108.

Khoury, Philip, *Syria and the French Mandate: The Politics of Arab Nationalism*, London: I. B. Tauris, 1987.

Kissinger, Henry, *Years of Renewal*, New York: Simon and Schuster, 1999.

———. *White House Years*, Boston: Little, Brown and Co., 1979.

Korn, David A., 'The Last Years of Mustafa Barzani', *Middle East Quarterly*, 1 (June 1994), pp. 12–27.

Kurdish Human Rights Project, *Enforcing the Charter for the Rights and Freedoms of Women in the Kurdish Regions and Diaspora*, London: Kurdish Human Rights Project, 2004.

Kurdistan Regional Government, 'President Barzani and Defense Secretary Gates in Erbil reaffirm long-term KRG-US relations', 11 December 2009.

———. *The Kurdistan Region: Invest in the Future*, Washington, DC: Newsdesk Media Inc., 2007.

KurdWatch. 'Who is the Syrian-Kurdish Opposition? The Development of Kurdish Parties, 1956–2011', Report 8, Berlin: European Centre for Kurdish Studies, 2011.

Kutschera, Chris, *Le Mouvement National Kurde*, Paris: Flammarion, 1979.

Landis, J. and J. Pace, 'The Syrian Opposition', *The Washington Quarterly*, 30, 1 (2006–2007).

Lang, Jennifer, 'Turkey's Counterterrorism Response to the Syrian Crisis', *Terrorism Monitor*, 11, 14 (12 July 2013), http://www.refworld.org…, last accessed 22 July 2013.

Lefèvre, Raphaël, *Ashes of Hama: The Muslim Brotherhood in Syria*, London: Hurst Publishers, 2012.

Lesch, David W., *Syria: The Fall of the House of Asad*, London and New Haven: Yale University Press, 2012.

Lewis, Bernard, *The Emergence of Modern Turkey*, 2nd ed., London: Oxford University Press, 1968.

Lowe, Robert, 'The *Serhildan* and the Kurdish National Story in Syria', in Robert Lowe and Gareth Stansfield (eds), *The Kurdish Policy Imperative*, London: Royal Institute of International Affairs, 2010, pp. 161–79.

———. 'Kurdish Nationalism in Syria', in Mohammed M. A. Ahmed and Michael M. Gunter (eds), *The Evolution of Kurdish Nationalism*, Costa Mesa, CA: Mazda Publishers, 2007, pp. 287–308.

Lynch, Maureen and Perveen Ali, 'Buried Alive: Stateless Kurds in Syria', Washington: Refugees International, 2006.

Malanczuk, Peter, *Akehurst's Modern Introduction to International Law*, 7th revised ed., London and New York: Routledge, 1997.

Marcus, Aliza, *Blood and Belief: The PKK and the Kurdish Fight for Independence*, New York and London: New York University Press, 2007.

McDowall, David, *A Modern History of the Kurds*, London and New York: I. B. Tauris, 1996.

Mella, Jawad, *The Colonial Policy of the Syrian Baath Party in Western Kurdistan*, London: Western Kurdistan Association, 2006.

Mojab, Shahrzad (ed.), *Women of a Non-State Nation: The Kurds*, Costa Mesa, CA: Mazda Publishers, 2001.

Montgomery, Harriet (Allsopp), *The Kurds of Syria: An Existence Denied*, Berlin: European Centre for Kurdish Studies, 2005.

Natali, Denise, *The Kurdish Quasi-State: Development and Dependency in Post-Gulf War Iraq*, Syracuse, NY: Syracuse University Press, 2010.

———. *The Kurds and the State: Evolving National Identity in Iraq, Turkey, and Iran*, Syracuse: Syracuse University Press, 2005.

Nazdar, Mustafa (Ismet Cheriff Vanly), 'The Kurds in Syria', in Gerard Chaliand, (ed.), *A People Without a Country: The Kurds and Kurdistan*, New York: Olive Branch Books, 1993, pp. 194–201.

O'Leary, Brendan, John McGarry and Khaled Salih (eds), *The Future of Kurdistan in Iraq*, Philadelphia: University of Pennsylvania Press, 2005.

Ocalan, Abdullah, *Prison Writings III: The Road Map to Negotiations*, trans. by Guneser, Havin, Cologne: International Initiative Edition, 2012.

———. *Prison Writings: The PKK and the Kurdish Question in the 21st Century*, trans. and edited by Happel, Klaus, London: Transmedia Publishing, 2011.

———. *Declaration on the Democratic Solution of the Kurdish Question*, London: Mesopotamian Publishers, 1999.

Olson, Robert, *The Emergence of Kurdish Nationalism and the Sheikh Said Rebellion, 1880–1925*, Austin: University of Texas Press, 1989.

Ozcan, Ali Kemal, *Turkey's Kurds: A Theoretical Analysis of the PKK and Abdullah Ocalan*, London and New York: Routledge, 2006.

Pope, Nicole, 'Kurdish women in Turkey: double discrimination', *Turkish Review*, 1 May 2013, http://www.turkishreview.org/tr/newsDetail_NewsById. action…, last accessed 20 Aug. 2013.

Public Papers of the Presidents of the United States: George Bush, 1991, vol. 1. Washington: Government Printing Office, 1992.

Randal, Jonathan C., *After Such Knowledge, What Forgiveness: My Encounters with Kurdistan*, New York: Farrar, Straus and Giroux, 1997.

Romano, David, *The Kurdish Nationalist Movement: Opportunity, Mobilization and Identity*, Cambridge: Cambridge University Press, 2006.

Savelsberg, Eva (KurdWatch, European Centre for Kurdish Studies, Berlin, Germany), e-mail interview with Michael Gunter, 26 August 2013.

Savelsberg, Eva and Jordi Tejel, 'The Syrian Kurds in "Transition to Somewhere"', in Mohammed M. A. Ahmed and Michael M. Gunter (eds), *The Kurdish Spring: Geopolitics Changes and the Kurds*, Costa Mesa, CA: Mazda Publishers, 2013, pp. 189–217.

Shaw, Stanford J. and Ezel Kural Shaw, *History of the Ottoman Empire and Modern Turkey*, Vol. II, *Reform, Revolution and Republic: The Rise of Modern Turkey, 1808–1975*, Cambridge: Cambridge University Press, 1977.

Shumilin, Alexander, 'Why Russia will not abandon Assad: the internal dynamics behind Russia's Syria policy', Center for Greater Middle East Conflicts at the Institute for the USA & Canada Studies (Russian Academy of Sciences), 15 August 2012, http://www.mesop.de/2012/08/17/why-russia…, last accessed 17 Aug. 2012.

Sinclair, Christian and Sirwan Kajjo, 'The evolution of Kurdish politics in Syria', *Middle East Research and Information Project*, 31 August 2011, http://www. merip.org/mero/mero083111?p…, last accessed 28 July 2013.

Starr, Stephen, *Revolt in Syria: Eye-Witness to the Uprising*, New York: Columbia University Press, 2012.

Strohmeier, Martin, *Crucial Images in the Presentation of Kurdish National Identity: Heroes and Patriots: Traitors and Foes*, Leiden and Boston: Brill, 2003.

Tejel, Jordi, *Syria's Kurds: History, Politics and Society*, London and New York: Routledge, 2009.

Torrey, Gordon, 'The Baath Ideology and Practice', *Middle East Journal*, 23 (Autumn 1969), pp. 445–70.

Unal, Mustafa Cosar, *Counterterrorism in Turkey: Policy Choices and Policy Effects toward the Kurdistan Workers' Party (PKK)*, London and New York: Routledge, 2012.

US Congress, Senate Committee on Foreign Relations, 'Syria Transition Support Act of 2013', S. Rept. 113–79, 113th Congress, 24 July 2013, http://beta. congress.gov/congressional-report/113th-congress/senate-report/79/1, last accessed 22 Sep. 2013.

————. *Civil War in Iraq: A Staff Report to the Committee on Foreign Relations*, by Peter W. Galbraith, 102nd Congress, 1st session, May 1991.

US Department of State, Bureau of Democracy, Human Rights, and Labor, *Country Reports on Human Rights Practices—2009*, 11 March 2010, http://www.state.gov..., last accessed 1 Mar. 2011.

Uslu, Emrullah, 'How Kurdish PKK militants are exploiting the crisis in Syria to achieve regional autonomy', *Terrorism Monitor*, 10, 7 (6 April 2012), pp. 8–11, http://www.jamestown.org/..., last accessed 6 July 2012.

Vanly, Ismet Cheriff, 'The Oppression of the Kurdish People in Syria', in Mohammed M. A. Ahmed and Michael M. Gunter (eds), *Kurdish Exodus: From Internal Displacement to Diaspora*, Sharon, MA: Ahmed Foundation for Kurdish Studies, 2002, pp. 49–62.

————. 'The Kurds in Syria and Lebanon', in Philip G. Kreyenbroek and Stefan Sperl (eds), *The Kurds: A Contemporary Overview*, London: Routledge, 1992, pp. 143–70.

Watts, Nicole F., *Activists in Office: Kurdish Politics and Protest in Turkey*, Seattle: University of Washington Press, 2010.

White, Benjamin, *The Emergence of Minorities in the Middle East: The Politics of Community in French Mandate Syria*, Edinburgh: Edinburgh University Press, 2011.

White, Damian F., *Bookchin: A Critical Appraisal*, London: Pluto Press, 2008.

White, Paul, *Primitive Rebels or Revolutionary Modernizers? The Kurdish National Movement in Turkey*, London and New York: Zed Books, 2000.

Wieland, Carsten, *Syria: A Decade of Lost Chances: Repression and Revolution from Damascus Spring to Arab Spring*, Seattle: Cune Press, 2012.

Yavuz, M. Hakan, *Secularism and Muslim Democracy in Turkey*, New York: Cambridge University Press, 2009.

Yildiz, Kerim, *The Kurds in Syria: The Forgotten People*, London: Pluto Press, 2005.

Yildiz, Kerim and Susan Breau, *The Kurdish Conflict: International Humanitarian Law and Post-Conflict Mechanisms*, London and New York: Routledge, 2010.

Yuksel, Metin, 'The Encounter of Kurdish Women with Nationalism in Turkey', *Middle Eastern Studies*, 42 (September 2006), pp. 777–802.

Zurcher, Erik J., *Turkey: A Modern History*, London: I. B. Tauris, 1994.

INDEX